# The Radical Teachings
of Jesus

Also by Derek J. Morris:

*The Radical Prayer*

To order, call 1-800-765-6955.

Visit us at

www.autumnhousepublishing.com

for information on other Autumn House® products.

# The Radical Teachings
# of Jesus

*The Radical Teachings of Jesus
will move you to the core of your being.*

—Mark Finley, Evangelist

*Derek J. Morris*

Autumn
House® Publishing
www.autumnhousepublishing.com
A Division of **REVIEW AND HERALD® PUBLISHING**
Since 1861

Published by Autumn House® Publishing, a division of Review and Herald® Publishing, Hagerstown, MD 21741-1119

This book was
Edited by Gerald Wheeler
Copyedited by Jan Schleifer
Designed by Trent Truman © Review and Herald
Cover photos by iStock.com/Harry Anderson
Typeset: Clearface 10/14.5

PRINTED IN U.S.A.

13  12  11  10  09          5  4  3  2  1

Library of Congress Cataloging-in-Publication Data
Morris, Derek John, 1954-     .
  The radical teachings of Jesus / Derek J. Morris.
      p. cm.
  Includes bibliographical references and index.
  1.  Jesus Christ—Teachings.  I. Title.
  BS2415.F57 2009
  232.9'54—dc22
                                   2009027865

ISBN 978-0-8127-0498-3 Hardcover
ISBN 978-0-8127-0506-5 Paperback

This book is

*Dedicated*

to Jesus—

The Way, the Truth, and the Life.


May His light shine brightly
in the heart and mind of every reader.

# In Praise of *The Radical Teachings of Jesus* . .
.

*When Jesus is the center of each Bible truth, hearts are*
*touched and lives are changed. Derek Morris uplifts the Jesus*
*of the New Testament in all of His richness and matchless*
*charms. But the gospel Jesus preached is not a soft, watered-*
*down version of easy believism.* The Radical Teachings of Jesus
*will move you to the core of your being.*

—*Mark Finley, Evangelist*

*This is a practical and powerful book on the life-changing*
*teachings of Jesus. I have known Derek Morris for many years,*
*and he has proved himself to be one of the most qualified*
*Christian leaders to write on this topic. As you read the deep*
*insights in this book, ask the Holy Spirit to work on your heart,*
*and you too will become radically changed for the better!*

—*Jerry Page, President Central California Conference*

The Radical Teachings of Jesus *is a book worth reading. It will*
*challenge your thinking and transform your life. Derek Morris*
*makes the teachings of Jesus practical and helps the reader*
*understand what the ministry of Jesus is all about.*

—*Jack Blanco, Th.D., Retired Dean of Theology*

# Acknowledgments

---

I want to express my appreciation to the numerous individuals who have provided encouragement and assistance in the development of this book:

To Mark and Teenie Finley, Todd Gessele, Gene Heinrich, Paul Johnson, Diane Levy, Dan Serns, Sue Walden, Larry Witzel and the team in Vancouver, WA, who provided the context for this manuscript to be born.

To Eve Parker and Nancy Vasquez—who provided invaluable feedback in the shaping and editing of the manuscript.

To my beloved wife, Bodil—who has always encouraged me to fix my eyes on Jesus, the Author and Finisher of our faith, and to boldly proclaim the radical teachings of Jesus.

Each of these individuals, along with others unnamed, encouraged me to sit at the feet of Jesus, listen carefully to His radical teachings, and share with others what I have learned .

Most of all, I want to thank Jesus, my Savior and Lord. I am fully persuaded that Jesus is all He claimed to be—Son of God, Messiah, Savior of the world, and soon-coming King! I echo the testimony of the great prophet John the Baptist: "Behold, the Lamb of God, who takes away the sin of the world. I have seen and testified that this is the Son of God!"

# *Contents*

---

# *Introduction*

————◆◆◆————

We are currently in the midst of an amazing miracle of God!
Since the publication of *The Radical Prayer* in 2008, more than
40,000 copies have already been printed. *The Radical Prayer* has
been translated into numerous languages, and thousands of study
groups across North America and around the world have begun
using *The Radical Prayer* DVD series.* But that is just the beginning.

Since I personally responded to the appeal of Jesus, crying out
to the Lord of the harvest to throw me out into His harvest, God
has been working in miraculous ways in my own life. In the
spring of 2009, I was thrown out to Vancouver, Washington, to
conduct a citywide series of meetings called The Radical Teachings of Jesus. The presentations stretched me to the limit—I felt
like a lamb, just like Jesus had foretold! In spite of some radical
challenges, I learned to radically depend upon the Lord of the
harvest. The result? I returned with radical joy, not only because
I saw with my own eyes that the harvest truly is great, but also
because I experienced the joy of salvation through Jesus Christ
our Lord in a deep and personal way.

This book is the result of that miracle. It is my prayer that as
you join me on a journey, exploring the radical teachings of
Jesus, your own life will be transformed.

————

* To learn more about *The Radical Prayer,* go to www.TheRadicalPrayer.com.

# 1

## What Jesus Taught About Himself

Have you heard the latest "news" about Jesus? Some say that He married Mary Magdalene and fathered a child. Others assert that Judas was the real hero in the gospel story. If you haven't studied the story of Jesus for yourself, you could easily get led astray. What did Jesus have to say about Himself, and are His radical claims true?

### Radical Claims of Jesus

Jesus was bold in His declarations about Himself. The apostle John remembered and recorded those radical claims:

- "I am the way, the truth, and the life. No one comes to the Father except through Me" (John 14:6).
- "I am the light of the world. He who follows Me shall not walk in darkness, but have the light of life" (John 8:12).

- "I am the bread of life. He who comes to Me shall never hunger, and he who believes in Me shall never thirst" (John 6:35).

- "I am the resurrection and the life. He who believes in Me, though he may die, he shall live. And whoever lives and believes in Me shall never die" (John 11:25, 26).

- "Most assuredly, I say to you, before Abraham was, I AM" (John 8:58).

- "My Father has been working until now, and I have been working" (John 5:17).

- "He who has seen Me has seen the Father" (John 14:9).

Radical claims indeed! The renowned Christian apologist C. S. Lewis was right when he asserted that Jesus didn't give us the option to recognize Him as merely a great moral teacher. Jesus was either a lunatic, totally out of touch with reality, a malicious deceiver intent on leading others astray, *or* He was and is who He claimed to be—the Messiah, the Savior, the Son of God.

Jesus left us with no doubt about whom He believed Himself to be: "I have come down from heaven, not to do My own will, but the will of Him who sent Me" (John 6:38). Of course, *anyone* can make outrageous claims like that. How do we know the radical claims of Jesus are true? To find an answer to that question, we must begin with the testimony of the early followers of Jesus.

## What His Followers Said

John the Baptist was one of the first to speak about Jesus. When he saw Jesus coming to the river Jordan to be baptized, he exclaimed, "Behold! The Lamb of God who takes away the sin of the world!" (John 1:29). After baptizing Jesus, John the Baptist gave this startling testimony: "I saw the Spirit descending from heaven like a dove, and He remained upon Him. . . . And I have seen and testified that this is the Son of God" (John 1:32-34). The viewpoint of John the Baptist was clear: he boldly declared that Jesus was the Son of God!

A godly woman named Martha, the sister of Mary and Lazarus, gave her testimony about Jesus. Martha and her siblings were close friends of Jesus. They knew Him well and loved Him. As she conversed with Jesus near the grave of her brother, Lazarus, Martha declared: "I believe that You are the Christ, the Son of God, who is to come into the world" (John 11:27).

Even skeptics experienced a radical change in their lives when they had a personal encounter with Jesus. When Nathanael's friend Philip said he had found the Messiah, a teacher from Nazareth, Nathanael replied, "Can anything good come out of Nazareth?" (John 1:46). But when Nathanael met Jesus face to face, he was convicted that Jesus was no ordinary man, and certainly not a lunatic or a malicious deceiver. Here is Nathanael's testimony: "Rabbi, You are the Son of God! You are the King of Israel!" (John 1:49).

Thomas was another skeptic who became a disciple of Jesus.

After the resurrection of Jesus, Thomas struggled to believe that He had actually risen from the dead. When he eventually met the risen Christ and saw Jesus with his own eyes and touched Him with his own hands, he exclaimed, "My Lord and my God!" (John 20:28).

You may have noticed that all the radical claims of Jesus cited above and all the quoted testimonies about Jesus come from the Gospel of John. One of the first disciples of Jesus, John, son of Zebedee, wrote his Gospel with the specific purpose of convincing people about who Jesus was. He proclaimed near the conclusion of his book: "And truly Jesus did many other signs in the presence of His disciples, which are not written in this book; *but these are written that you may believe that Jesus is the Christ, the Son of God*, and that believing you may have life in His name" (John 20:30, 31, emphasis supplied).

## Authenticity of John's Testimony

John's Gospel gives such a sophisticated picture of Jesus that many liberal scholars question its authenticity. They suggest that the Gospel of John must have evolved through a century or more, and propose that it was written late in the second century A.D., long after John's death. They say the Gospel of John may contain a few fragments of true tradition, but in its present form it is not an authentic testimony from the disciple "whom Jesus loved" (John 21:20).

However, an archaeological discovery during the twentieth century provided evidence reaffirming a late first-century date for the writing of the Gospel of John, thus supporting its authenticity as the work of the aged apostle John. In 1920 a collection of papyri purchased in Egypt went to the John Rylands Library in England. Scholars translated and first published one papyrus fragment from that collection in 1935. It became known as the Rylands Papyrus 457, or P52. Paleographers—scholars who specialize in dating documents based on writing styles—were excited to date this ancient papyrus as early second century, perhaps around A.D. 125. On it was a portion of the Gospel of John. Already published in codex (like a modern paged book) form rather than a conventional scroll, the evidence clearly pointed to a late first century date for the writing of John's Gospel, just as Christians had believed through the centuries. I am convinced that God directed the discovery of that ancient papyrus to strengthen the faith of Christians and to affirm the authenticity of John's witness.

Perhaps you are wondering what was written on that papyrus fragment. It was portions of John 18:31-33 on one side and parts of John 18:37, 38 on the reverse side. "Then Pilate said to them, 'You take Him and judge Him according to your law.' Therefore the Jews said to him, 'It is not lawful for us to put anyone to death,' that the saying of Jesus might be fulfilled which He spoke, signifying by what death He would die.

Then Pilate entered the Praetorium again, called Jesus, and said to Him, 'Are You the King of the Jews?'" (John 18:31-33).

On the reverse side of the fragment we find additional portions of the conversation between Pilate and Jesus. "Pilate therefore said to Him, 'Are You a king then?' Jesus answered, 'You say rightly that I am a king. For this cause I was born, and for this cause I have come into the world, that I should bear witness to the truth. Everyone who is of the truth hears My voice.' Pilate said to Him, 'What is truth?' And when he had said this, he went out again to the Jews, and said to them, 'I find no fault in Him at all'" (verses 37, 38).

"Everyone who is of the truth hears My voice!" We all have the power to choose the one to whom we are going to listen. Distractions and fanciful fabrications constantly surround us. It's part of the great struggle between good and evil. But God has provided compelling evidence that the testimonies about Jesus are reliable and that His radical claims are true!

## The Testimony of Saul

One of the most compelling testimonies regarding the truth about Jesus comes from Saul of Tarsus, once a fierce and ruthless enemy of Jesus and all who followed Him. Saul, later called Paul, told the Jewish king Agrippa: "Indeed, I myself thought I must do many things contrary to the name of Jesus of Nazareth. This I also did in Jerusalem, and many of the saints I shut up in prison, having received authority from the chief priests; and when they were put to death, I cast my vote against them. And I punished them often in every synagogue and compelled them to blaspheme; and being exceedingly enraged against them, I persecuted them even to foreign cities" (Acts 26:9-11).

Saul had been a witness to the stoning of Stephen, one of the followers of Jesus. That execution indelibly imprinted itself on Saul's memory, and the convictions generated by Stephen's death would be with Saul forever. Stephen had just given a powerful testimony about Jesus Christ before the Sanhedrin, the ruling council of the Jews. The author of the book of Acts records that "when they heard these things they were cut to the heart, and they gnashed at him with their teeth. But he, being full of the Holy Spirit, gazed into heaven and saw the glory of God, and Jesus standing at the right hand of God, and said, 'Look! I see the heavens opened and the Son of Man standing at the right hand of God!' Then they cried out with a loud voice, stopped their ears, and ran at him with one accord; and they cast him out of the city and stoned him. And the witnesses laid down their clothes at the feet of a young man named Saul. And they stoned Stephen as he was calling on God and saying, 'Lord Jesus, receive my spirit.' Then he knelt down and cried out with a loud voice, 'Lord, do not charge them with this sin.' And when he had said this, he fell asleep" (Acts 7:54-60).

Not long after this, Saul was on his way to Damascus with authorization from the high priest in Jerusalem. He intended to arrest any followers of Jesus he found there and bring them back to Jerusalem in chains. But God had other plans. "As he journeyed he came near Damascus, and suddenly a light shone around him from heaven. Then he fell to the ground, and heard a voice saying to him, 'Saul, Saul, why are you persecuting Me?' And he said, 'Who are You, Lord?' Then the Lord said, 'I am Jesus, whom you are persecuting'" (Acts 9:3-5).

That encounter with the risen Christ changed the course of his life. Saul the persecutor became Paul the devoted follower of Jesus. He began boldly to declare that Jesus was the Christ, the Son of God. He healed the sick and cast out demons in Jesus' name, just like the other apostles, and he joyfully looked forward to "the blessed hope and glorious appearing of our great God and Savior Jesus Christ" (Titus 2:13).

## The Testimony of Peter and John

As Jesus' disciples Peter and John approached the Temple in Jerusalem they saw a crippled man begging there. "Now Peter and John went up together to the temple at the hour of prayer, the ninth hour. And a certain man lame from his mother's womb was carried, whom they laid daily at the gate of the temple which is called Beautiful, to ask alms from those who entered the temple; who, seeing Peter and John about to go into the temple, asked for alms. And fixing his eyes on him, with John, Peter said, 'Look at us.' So he gave them his attention, expecting to receive something from them. Then Peter said,

'Silver and gold I do not have, but what I do have I give you: In the name of Jesus Christ of Nazareth, rise up and walk.' And he took him by the right hand and lifted him up, and immediately his feet and ankle bones received strength. So he, leaping up, stood and walked and entered the temple with them—walking, leaping, and praising God. And all the people saw him walking and praising God. Then they knew that it was he who sat begging alms at the Beautiful Gate of the temple; and they were filled with wonder and amazement at what had happened to him" (Acts 3:1-10).

The people who witnessed the incident were astonished. When Peter saw the reaction of the crowd, he said: "Men of Israel, why do you marvel at this? Or why look so intently at us, as though by our own power or godliness we had made this man walk? The God of Abraham, Isaac, and Jacob, the God of our fathers, glorified His Servant Jesus, whom you delivered up and denied in the presence of Pilate, when he was determined to let Him go. But you denied the Holy One and the Just, and asked for a murderer to be granted to you, and killed the Prince of life, whom God raised from the dead, of which we are witnesses. And His name, through faith in His name, has made this man strong, whom you see and know. Yes, the faith which comes through Him has given him this perfect soundness in the presence of you all. Yet now, brethren, I know that you did it in ignorance, as did also your rulers. But those things which God foretold by the mouth of all His prophets, that the Christ would suffer, He has thus fulfilled. Repent therefore and be converted, that your sins may be blotted out, so that times of refreshing may come from the presence of the Lord, and that He may send Jesus Christ, who was preached to you before" (Acts 3:12-20). Peter's testimony, both in words and actions, boldly confirmed that the radical claims of Jesus were true. Jesus is the Christ, the Holy One!

## The Testimony of Evil Spirits

During the ministry of Jesus evil spirits also supported the radical claims that Jesus made about Himself. On one occasion, when He was speaking in the synagogue in Capernaum, a demon-possessed man exclaimed, "Let us alone! What have we to do with You, Jesus of Nazareth? Did You come to destroy us? I know who You are—the Holy One of God!" (Mark 1:24). Jesus did not challenge the evil spirit's testimony but simply rebuked it, saying, "Be quiet, and come out of him!" (verse 25). Mark records that after the unclean spirit had convulsed the demon-possessed man and cried out with a loud voice, it left him. "Then they were all amazed, so that they questioned among themselves, saying, 'What is this? What new doctrine is this? For with authority He commands even the unclean spirits, and they obey Him.' And immediately His fame spread throughout all the region around Galilee" (verses 27, 28).

The book of Acts records many stories of people being set free from the control of evil spirits by the power of Jesus' name. In the city of Philippi a young demon-possessed girl followed Paul and Silas around, shouting, "These men are the servants of the Most High God, who proclaim to us the way of salvation" (Acts 16:17). While her testimony endorsed the radical claims that Jesus had made about Himself, Paul realized that such constant verbal harassment was more of a distraction than a help. So Paul confronted the evil spirit: "I command you in the name of Jesus Christ to come out of her" (verse 18). The being could not resist the power of Jesus' name and had no choice but to leave.

Such stories confirm that Jesus was no ordinary man, and that He was certainly not a lunatic or a malicious deceiver. Because Jesus was and is all that He claimed to be, we find incredible power in His name. But I must warn you that it's not enough to know *about* Jesus. You need to know Him personally if you expect to experience His power in your life.

A story recorded in Acts 19:13-16 illustrates this very point. Some of the itinerant Jewish exorcists tried to cast out evil spirits in the name of Jesus even though they did not believe in Him themselves. When seven sons of Sceva, a Jewish chief priest, tried to perform an exorcism in the name of Jesus, the evil spirit replied, "Jesus I know, and Paul I know; but who are you?" (Acts 19:15) Then the demon-possessed man leaped on them, overpowered them, and beat them, so that they ran out of that house naked and bleeding.

That startling story ought to convince you that it is not enough to know *about* Jesus. You need a personal relationship with Him.

When you are personally connected to Jesus, you will find healing and freedom such as you've never experienced before.

But all these testimonies are from long ago. What about the twenty-first century? Do we see evidence even today that the radical claims of Jesus are true? Yes! In fact, the transformation of lives continues to be the greatest support of those claims. Fanciful fabrications that seek to undermine or deny the truth about Jesus will help no one, but when you meet Jesus Christ personally— even today—your life will never be the same again. Let those who scoff about Jesus and religion mock. Let the critics ridicule. But they cannot save you or heal you. Nor can they set you free from the things that cripple your life. Only Jesus can do that.

## The Testimony of Will

In the fall of 2008 I had the privilege of conducting a series of religious meetings in Orlando, Florida, with internationally known evangelist Mark Finley. We saw many miracles of lives transformed by the power of Jesus during those sessions. I remember one young man named Will, who was 25 years old. He had dropped out of high school at age 16, and by now his life was going nowhere. In fact, he had been an alcoholic for the past seven years. The first night he came to the meetings, he was experiencing a hangover. Later he said that the only reason he attended was that his mom had dragged him there! As Will began hearing about Jesus night after night, it radically transformed his life. He has been sober since that life-changing encounter with Jesus and is now an active witness for the One who delivered him from the bondage of sin. Will's story finds itself repeated again and again in the lives of young and old who experience a personal life-changing encounter with Jesus.

Jesus still invites people today, "Come to Me, all you who labor and are heavy laden, and I will give you rest. Take My yoke upon you and learn from Me, for I am gentle and lowly in heart, and you will find rest for your souls" (Matthew 11:28, 29). Jesus can give you rest for your soul because He is no ordinary man. He isn't just a great moral teacher, and He certainly isn't a deluded lunatic or a malicious deceiver. Jesus is the Christ, the Son of the living God.

Do you need peace in your life? Are you looking for freedom from the chains that bind you? The good news is that Jesus can make you whole. Christ can set you free. No fanciful fabrication could ever do that.

# 2

## What Jesus Taught About the Scriptures

According to an article I downloaded from the American Humanist Association, I am a deluded fool. The author of the article—the president of a local chapter of the American Humanist Association—would probably label me "a promoter of deceptive and destructive teachings." In an article entitled "Some Reasons Why Humanists Reject the Bible" the author makes this bold assertion:

"Humanists reject the claim that the Bible is the word of God. They are convinced the book was written solely by humans in an ignorant, superstitious, and cruel age. They believe that because the writers of the Bible lived in an unenlightened era, the book contains many errors and harmful teachings."[1]

Perhaps even more troubling than his statement is the fact that even some *Christians* are losing confidence in the Scriptures. Many Christian theologians have embraced a methodology in which "critical reason decides what is reality in the Bible, and what cannot be reality."[2]

## Scripture Discounted as Myth

The Scriptures are being demythologized. Whatever the reader decides is incredible gets discarded. Many have abandoned the Genesis creation account as unscientific. Others interpret miracles according to what seems reasonable. Some of you have probably heard the "rational" explanation for the feeding of the 5,000 by Jesus.[3] According to those who adopt such an approach to the Scriptures, it is irrational to believe that Jesus could feed 5,000 men, plus women and children, with five loaves and two fish. They say what really happened was this: everyone actually had food with them, but no one wanted to share it. When the young lad demonstrated a willingness to share his lunch with Jesus, his action touched the hearts of the people, and they all shared their food with one another. Isn't that a miracle? The miracle of love!

Well, I believe love *is* a miracle. But that's *not* what the Bible says happened. The crowd didn't want to honor the little boy for his generous spirit. They wanted to make *Jesus* king. Even the enemies of Jesus could not deny the supernatural signs and wonders He performed. Yet today many try to explain them away or discard them as myths. They do not believe that the testimony of Scripture is reliable.

So what is the truth about the Scriptures, and how should we respond to the erosion of confidence in them? If we choose to base our convictions on current popular opinion, we're in serious trouble. Let me suggest that it would be wise to consider carefully what Jesus taught about the Scriptures.

## The Word of God

Jesus declared that the Scriptures are more than a helpful collection of religious ideas. They are more than words of human beings *about* God. The Scriptures *are* the inspired Word of God. When Satan tempted Jesus in the wilderness, He responded by quoting from Scripture. He said, "It is written, 'Man shall not live by bread alone; but by every word that proceeds from the mouth of God'" (Matthew 4:4, quoting Deuteronomy 8:3).

How do we receive that divine Word? Through the oral and written testimony of the prophets. That is the radical teaching that Jesus shared with His disciples, one of whom wrote later: "And so we have the prophetic word confirmed, which you do well to heed as a light that shines in a dark place, until the day dawns and the morning star rises in your hearts; knowing this first, that no prophecy of Scripture is of any private interpretation, for prophecy never came by the will of man, but holy men of God spoke as they were moved by the Holy Spirit" (2 Peter 1:19-21).

## Old Testament Stories

By faith Jesus accepted the testimony of Scripture as the Word of God. He had undoubtedly heard the story of the young prophet Jeremiah. The Lord called Jeremiah to be a prophet, and Jeremiah responded, "Ah, Lord God! Behold, I cannot speak, for I am a youth" (Jeremiah 1:6).

But the Lord said to Jeremiah, "Do not say, 'I am a youth,' for you shall go to all to whom I send you, and whatever I command you, you shall speak. Do not be afraid of their faces, for I am with you to deliver you" (verses 7, 8). Then God touched the young prophet's mouth and said, "Behold, I have put My words in your mouth" (verse 9).

For Jesus, the testimony of prophets such as Jeremiah was much more than helpful religious counsel—it was the Word of God, transmitted through a human instrument.

Many unbelievers—and, sadly, even some Christians—do not regard the early chapters of the book of Genesis as reliable history, but Jesus accepted them as the trustworthy Word of God. Jesus said, "Have you not read that He who made them at the beginning 'made them male and female'" (Matthew 19:4). Jesus also spoke of the blood of righteous Abel (Matthew 23:35) and the days of Noah, when he "entered the ark, and the flood came and destroyed them all" (Luke 17:27).

Why did Jesus believe those events really happened? He couldn't prove their historicity based on human logic or reason. Rather, Jesus by faith accepted the Scriptures as the dependable Word of God. That's why He could recount the story of Jonah being in the belly of a great fish for three days and three nights as a historical fact. It doesn't make sense to human reason. From a human perspective the story of Jonah sounds like a preposterous fish story. But Jesus by faith accepted the story as a historical fact because Scripture recorded it (see Matthew 12:40).

## Moses and King David

Revisionists and biblical minimalists say Bible characters such as Moses and King David never existed. They are simply a fabrication of those who desire to promote a political agenda. Jesus, on the other hand, believed in the historicity of Moses and of King David. Jesus told of Moses lifting up the serpent in the wilderness (John 3:14), and He also spoke of King David, quoting the words of David recorded in Psalm 110:1 as being spoken "by the Holy Spirit" (Mark 12:36).

Jesus believed and taught that the Bible was more than just human words about God. The Scriptures were and are the inspired Word of God, filled with His wisdom and power. May it be said of us, as the apostle Paul declared of believers in the Greek city of Thessalonica, "We also thank God without ceasing, because when you received the Word of God which you heard from us, you welcomed it not as the word of men, but as it is in truth, the Word of God, which also effectively works in you who believe" (1 Thessalonians 2:13).

## Defense Against the Enemy

A second important truth that Jesus taught about the Scriptures is that they are a defense against the forces of evil. When Jesus went into the wilderness after His baptism, He responded to every attack by Satan with the Word of God. When tempted to turn stones into bread, Jesus said, "It is written, 'Man shall not live by bread alone, but by every word that proceeds from the mouth of God.'" (Matthew 4:4, quoting Deuteronomy 8:3).

After Satan urged Him to presume upon the mercy of God, Jesus replied, "It is written again, 'You shall not tempt the Lord your God'" (Matthew 4:7, quoting Deuteronomy 6:16). Again, when Satan tried to get Jesus to bow down and worship him through the deceptive promise that he would give the whole world to Him, Jesus replied, "Away with you, Satan! For it is written, 'You shall worship the Lord your God, and Him only you shall serve'" (Matthew 4:10, quoting Deuteronomy 6:13).

How was Jesus able to respond to each temptation with the Word of God? Did He have a scroll or two hidden under His cloak? No. Because He believed that the Scriptures were the Word of God, He had stored them in His heart. He took time to memorize and internalize the Word of God. Then, when the enemy attacked, Jesus had a defense against him. The Savior demonstrated in His encounter with Satan the truth of the Word of God recorded in Ephesians 6:17: "The sword of the Spirit . . . is the word of God."

The Greek noun translated "word" both in Matthew 4:4[4] and Ephesians 6:17[5] is not the common word *logos*.[6] Rather, it is the

Greek noun *rhēma*, which implies a specific word or saying. When Satan challenged Him, Jesus didn't just hold up the Bible or a Bible scroll as if it were some kind of lucky charm and say, "The Bible, the Bible, the Bible." No, Jesus responded with *specific* words from the Scriptures.

So why are the Scriptures a defense against Satan? Because he is a liar and a deceiver, but the Word of God is truth. So when Satan comes to you and says, "You're a sinner. You're a loser. You might as well just give up and be damned," the Word of God tells you the truth: "If we confess our sins, He is faithful and just to forgive us our sins and to cleanse us from *all* unrighteousness" (1 John 1:9). The truth of the Word of God dispels his lie.

When Satan tries to intimidate you and fill you with fear, the Word of God tells you the truth: "Fear not, for I am with you; be not dismayed, for I am your God. I will strengthen you, yes, I will help you, I will uphold you with My righteous right hand" (Isaiah 41:10).

Or when Satan seeks to discourage you because the path ahead seems uncertain, the Word of God reminds you of the truth: "I will instruct you and teach you in the way you should go; I will guide you with My eye" (Psalm 32:8).

## Defense Lessons

The Word of God is a defense against the evil enemy. I remember an incident that happened when I was about 10 years old that confirmed this radical teaching of Jesus. I lived about a mile from the campus of Newbold College, a small Christian college in the village of Binfield, England. It was a Friday evening, and I had gone to a vespers program at the church. I'm not sure why my family allowed me to walk home by myself. In retrospect it seems a little dangerous, but we lived less than a mile from the campus, down a country road. On my way home, as I was passing the ruins of an old building, I heard a blood-curdling scream. I was terrified! Even as a 10-year-old I clearly saw the situation as an attempt by supernatural agencies to intimidate me. But then something amazing happened. The words of Psalm 23 came into my mind. I had memorized Psalm 23 as a young child, and I embraced those words, not simply as the words of David, but as the Word of God.

"The Lord is my shepherd; I shall not want. . . . Though I walk through the valley of the shadow of death, I will fear no evil" (verses 1-4, KJV). As I repeated that psalm, God's Word became to me "the sword of the Spirit" (Ephesians 6:17). The Lord kept me in perfect peace as my mind focused on Him (see Isaiah 26:3). That promise was true the day the prophet wrote it down, and it is still true today! I learned that dark night more than 40 years ago, and many times since then, that the Scriptures *are* a defense against the enemy.

Some years ago I got a phone call asking if I could pray a blessing over someone's house. Apparently, a woman named Glenda[7] had recently been widowed, and the superstition of her culture taught that the departed spirit of her dead husband would visit the house for 40 days after his death. About a week after her husband's death, Glenda began to hear rapping sounds in the part of the house where her husband had died. Although an educated woman with a Ph.D. in nutritional science and a competent professional, she didn't know how to handle this supernatural phenomenon. As I prepared to go to Glenda's house, I felt impressed to take one of my wife's Scripture song CDs with me—*Wells of Salvation*. I encouraged Glenda to play it in her home and to hide in her heart the Word of God contained in the songs. The next morning I received an excited call from Glenda. "The rapping is gone!" The power of the Word of God had expelled from her house the evil spirit harassing her!

Jesus was the Word of God made flesh, and His Word is still a defense against Satan. In fact, I propose to you that we need the Word of God as a weapon against him now more than at any other time in the history of our world. We are living in troubled times as we see the fulfillment of the prophecy of John in the book of Revelation that "the devil has come down to you, having great wrath, because he knows that he has a short time" (Revelation 12:12).

One of the best ways to instill God's Word in your heart is through Scripture songs. My wife and I sing them for family worship. We believe, as did Jesus, that the Scriptures are the Word of God and a protection against evil, and we encourage you to place God's Word in your heart.

## Testimony About Jesus Christ

It is possible, however, to memorize a few important passages from the Scripture and yet overlook their most important truth. Religious leaders in Jesus' day thought they could find life by knowing the Scriptures. They became experts in what the Scriptures said. Tragically, in their lifelong quest for biblical knowledge, they missed the whole purpose of God's Word. Jesus said, "You search the Scriptures, for in them you think you have eternal life; and these are they which testify of Me. But you are not willing to come to Me that you may have life" (John 5:39, 40).

What a bold claim! Jesus said, "The Scriptures are a testimony about Me!" That's the third important truth Jesus taught about the Scriptures. When the risen Jesus gave a Bible study to the two disciples He met on the road to Emmaus, Luke records that "beginning at Moses and all the Prophets, He expounded to them in all the Scriptures the things concerning Himself" (Luke 24:27).

The purpose for reading the Bible is not just to gain more information. Nor is it just to learn more about Jesus. Satan and those angels who followed him in his rebellion have lots of Bible knowledge and lots of information about Jesus. Many of those who will be excluded from the kingdom of heaven are well informed about Jesus Christ. Rather, Jesus says that the reason we should study the Scriptures is to come to know Him personally.

The apostle John tells us that he wrote his Gospel for that very reason. "And truly Jesus did many other signs in the presence of His disciples, which are not written in this book; but these are written that you may believe that Jesus is the Christ, the Son of God, and that believing you may have life in His name" (John 20:30, 31). We read the Scriptures that we might do more than just know *about* Jesus. We want to have an intimate relationship with Him whom to know is life eternal (see John 17:3).

Jesus taught that the Scriptures are the Word of God, that they are a defense against the enemy, and that they are a testimony about Him. We may never have answers to all our questions, but we're not saved by having all the answers. Rather, salvation comes from knowing Jesus, our Savior and Lord. Once we have a personal, saving relationship with Him, we will be ready to listen attentively to the radical teachings of Jesus, and we will desire to live in harmony with all He taught.

---

[1] www.americanhumanist.org/humanism/thebible.html.

[2] Eta Linnemann, *Historical Criticism of the Bible: Methodology or Ideology?* (Grand Rapids: Baker Book House, 1990), p. 88.

[3] This remarkable miracle appears in all four Gospels: Matthew 14:13-21; Mark 6:35-44; Luke 9:10-17; John 6:1-14.

[4] "Man shall not live by bread alone, but by every *word* that proceeds from the mouth of God" (Matthew 4:4).

[5] "The sword of the Spirit, which is the *word* of God" (Ephesians 6:17).

[6] The Greek noun *logos* appears in Hebrews 4:12, which states, "The *word* of God is living and powerful, and sharper than any two-edged sword."

[7] Glenda is a pseudonym.

# 3

## What Jesus Taught About Salvation

You probably received the same e-mail that showed up in my in-box some months ago. It recorded the results of a biblical knowledge test supposedly given to several elementary school children. Their answers, some of which appear below, reveal some rather confused ideas about the Bible:

- Noah's wife was Joan of Ark.
- Lot's wife was a pillar of salt by day and a ball of fire by night.
- Moses went to the top of Mount Cyanide to get the Ten Commandments.
- The seventh commandment is "Thou shalt not admit adultery."
- Joshua led the Hebrews in the battle of Geritol.
- Solomon had 300 wives and 700 porcupines.
- Samson defeated the Philistines with the axe of the apostles.

• The epistles were the wives of the apostles.

While the e-mail is probably a humorous hoax, it still illustrates a troublesome trend in our culture. We are rapidly becoming a biblically illiterate society, with our children growing up knowing less and less about the great stories of the Bible. It's sad because those stories help us to understand the important teachings of the Bible, which in turn enables us to learn valuable lessons for our own lives today (see Romans 15:4).

The passage of Scripture that we will study now is a case in point. In chapter 1 we discovered the radical claims that Jesus made about Himself. In chapter 2, we examined the radical teaching of Jesus about the Scriptures. Now we're going to consider what Jesus taught about salvation.

## Jesus Teaches Nicodemus

Nicodemus was a member of the Sanhedrin, the Jewish ruling council. He came to talk to Jesus one night. While he was personally convicted that Jesus was a teacher sent from God, he was not quite ready to declare himself an open follower of Him. During the course of their conversation Jesus shared with Nicodemus a radical teaching about salvation: "And as Moses lifted up the serpent in the wilderness, even so must the Son of Man be lifted up, that whoever believes in Him should not perish but have eternal life. For God so loved the world that He gave His only begotten Son, that whoever believes in Him should not perish but have everlasting life" (John 3:14–16).

The incident that Jesus alluded to had happened more than 1,400 years earlier while the children of Israel were on their way to the Promised Land. We find this significant Bible story in the Old Testament book of Numbers. Aaron, the brother of Moses, had just died. The children of Israel were making a lengthy detour around the territory of the Edomites, and once again they had begun complaining against God.

"Then they journeyed from Mount Hor by the Way of the Red Sea, to go around the land of Edom; and the soul of the people became very discouraged on the way. And the people spoke against God and against Moses: 'Why have you brought us up out of Egypt to die in the wilderness? For there is no food and no water, and our soul loathes this worthless bread'" (Numbers 21:4, 5).

God's people were focusing on their difficulties rather than on their Deliverer. Even the blessings of God, including the daily manna which God had provided for them, were a cause for complaint. "Our soul loathes this worthless bread," they brashly complained.

## Fiery Serpents

The very next verse presents a picture that is troubling to many people. "So the Lord sent fiery serpents among the people, and they bit the people; and many of the people of Israel died" (Numbers 21:6). A person could easily create a horrible picture of God from just that one verse—a mean-spirited, vindictive Deity who zaps people when they step out of line. But is that an accurate description of the character of God? Not if you believe the words of

Jesus, who said, "If you have seen Me, you have seen the Father" (John 14:9, CEV). Jesus told us, "God so loved the world . . ." (John 3:16). So what's happening here in Numbers 21:6?

Moses had recently reminded the children of Israel that the Lord had led them "through that great and terrible wilderness, in which were fiery serpents and scorpions and thirsty land where there was no water" (Deuteronomy 8:15). Although dangers and difficulties surrounded them, the Lord had provided for them. He had given them food in the form of manna, had provided water from the rock, and had protected them from the fiery serpents and scorpions. But then they complained against God and against Moses. "Why have you brought us up out of Egypt to die in the wilderness?" (Numbers 21:5).

The unspoken message was clear. "We wish we weren't Your people. Please just leave us alone." God honored their request. He allowed them to face life and death without Him. As a natural consequence of their willful separation from God, those same fiery serpents from which He had graciously protected them during their long desert journey now bit the people. Can you imagine the ensuing panic within the camp of Israel? There they were, out in the middle of a hostile desert with nowhere to hide. Even if they somehow managed to survive through the day without receiving a venomous bite, they still had to face the greater uncertainty of making it through the night unscathed. Loud screams spread all through the camp as the serpents bit more and still more of the people. Many Israelites perished.

We don't know how long the complaining lasted, but the children of Israel finally came to their senses and sent representatives to talk with Moses. "Therefore the people came to Moses, and said, 'We have sinned, for we have spoken against the Lord and against you; pray to the Lord that He take away the serpents from us.' So Moses prayed for the people" (verse 7).

## Serpent on a Pole

The Lord replied to Moses, "Make a fiery serpent, and set it on a pole; and it shall be that everyone who is bitten, when he looks at it, shall live" (verse 8). It didn't seem to make any sense at all. How could looking at a replica of the *problem* provide a *solution*? The Lord was asking the children of Israel to reaffirm their commitment to Him as their God through a simple act of obedience.

"So Moses made a bronze serpent, and put it on a pole; and so it was, if a serpent had bitten anyone, when he looked at the bronze serpent, he lived" (verse 9). It was a look of dependence—trusting the Lord to be faithful to His promise—and all who looked lived.

I now imagine another cry going up in the camp. Not one of death, but of life. Instead of an expression of despair it was one of hope. "The Lord has told us to look at the bronze serpent and we will live. Look and live! Look and live!"

Undoubtedly some saw no sense either in God's instructions or the invitation. So instead of looking toward God's provision, they turned away, and consequently died in their rebellion. But some repentant sinners had the courage to believe the Word of God—to do what God asked them to do. Through a simple act of faith, perhaps with the assistance of those around them, they made their way to the center of the camp. There they gazed in faith at the bronze serpent, in simple obedience to the word of God, and lived!

## Lifted Up

Hundreds of years later Jesus said to Nicodemus, "As Moses lifted up the serpent in the wilderness, even so must the Son of Man be lifted up" (John 3:14). What did He mean by that? On another occasion Jesus said, "When you lift up the Son of Man, then you will know that I am He, and that I do nothing of Myself; but as My Father taught Me, I speak these things. And He who sent Me is with Me. The Father has not left Me alone, for I always do those things that please Him" (John 8:28, 29).

But we still haven't answered the question: What is this "lifting up" of the Son of man that must happen? Jesus said, "And I, if I am lifted up from the earth, will draw all peoples to Myself" (John 12:32). Under the guidance of the Holy Spirit the apostle John added an inspired commentary: "This He said, signifying by what death He would die" (verse 33).

Notice carefully the words of Jesus. "Even so *must* the Son of Man be lifted up." Why? Because the death of Jesus on the cross is not just something tacked on to the gospel story. It is, rather, at the very center of God's saving activity. That's why the apostle Paul declared: "God forbid that I should boast except in the cross of our Lord Jesus Christ" (Galatians 6:14), and "I determined not to know anything among you except Jesus Christ and Him crucified" (1 Corinthians 2:2). "For the message of the cross is foolishness to those who are perishing, but to us who are being saved it is the power of God" (1 Corinthians 1:18).

Jesus explained to Nicodemus: "And as Moses lifted up the serpent in the wilderness, even so must the Son of Man be lifted up, that whoever believes in Him should not perish but have eternal life. For God so loved the world that He gave His only begotten Son, that whoever believes in Him should not perish but have everlasting life. *For God did not send His Son into the world to condemn the world, but that the world through Him might be saved*" (John 3:14-17).

When people look to Jesus in faith, they find life—abundant, in all its fullness, and everlasting. The cry needs to go out, just as it did in the camp of Israel: not a wail of death, but an announcement of life; not of despair, but of hope. Look to the provision God has made. Look to Jesus in faith, and live!

## The Rich Young Ruler

Unfortunately, some persist in rejecting God's gracious offer. Just like those who chose not to look at the bronze snake, some even during the ministry of Jesus spurned salvation. Luke records the story of a Jewish official who came to Jesus: "Now a certain ruler asked Him, saying, 'Good Teacher, what shall I do to inherit eternal life?'" (Luke 18:18).

That's a strange question, but it reveals a great deal about the rich young leader. First, notice what he called Jesus: "Good Teacher." It's a polite title, but it reveals a lack of commitment on the part of the speaker. Some called Jesus "Master," others "Lord." This young man simply addresses Him as "Teacher," perhaps throwing in the word "good" in order to earn some favor.

But Jesus was not impressed. "Why do you call Me good? No one is good but One, that is, God" (verse 19). In other words, "Are you willing to recognize Me for who I am? I am indeed the one who alone can be called good."

Something else reveals much about the young man. He asked: "What shall I do to inherit eternal life?" You can't *do* anything to inherit something. Inheritance comes because of who you are. You don't *do* anything to inherit eternal life—it's a gift to those who have a relationship with Jesus, to those who look to Him in faith. If anything gets in the way of our relationship with Jesus—our skepticism, our pride, our possessions, whatever—we need to let it go and choose to look to Jesus in faith, and live. Unfortunately, the rich young ruler couldn't let go of his possessions, and sadly, we never hear of him again.

## Zacchaeus

The response of another rich man is quite different: "Then Jesus entered and passed through Jericho. Now behold, there was a man named Zacchaeus who was a chief tax collector, and he was rich. And he sought to see who Jesus was, but could not because of the crowd, for he was of short stature. So he ran ahead and climbed up into a sycamore tree to see Him, for He was going to pass that way. And when Jesus came to the place, He looked up and saw him, and said to him, 'Zacchaeus, make haste and come down, for today I must stay at your house.' So he made haste and came down, and received Him joyfully. But when they saw it, they all complained, saying, 'He has gone to be a guest with a man who is a sinner.' Then Zacchaeus stood and said to the Lord, 'Look, Lord, I give half of my goods to the poor; and if I have taken anything from anyone by false accusation, I restore fourfold.' And Jesus said to him, 'Today salvation has come to this house, because he also is a son of Abraham; for the Son of Man has come to seek and to save that which was lost'" (Luke 19:1-10).

Jericho undoubtedly had many local tax collectors because of its strategic location on a trade route, and Zacchaeus was the *chief* tax collector. Probably he wore luxurious robes and sandals made of the finest leather. Yet none of his fine attire mattered as he climbed up that sycamore tree. Just like the young ruler, Zacchaeus was a rich man seeking to speak with Jesus, but that's where the similarities end. Instead of referring to Jesus as "Good Teacher," Zacchaeus called Him "Lord." Unlike the Jewish leader who turned away sorrowfully, Zacchaeus received Jesus joyfully. And instead of hoarding his money, Zacchaeus gave it away. "Look, Lord, I give half of my goods to the poor; and if I have taken anything from anyone by false accusation, I restore fourfold" (verse 8).

Jesus told him, "Today salvation has come to this house." Why? Because Zacchaeus gave half of what he owned to the poor? No. Why then? Because he demonstrated humility by restoring fourfold to anyone he had wronged? Again, no. His actions were only evidence of his salvation, not its cause. Salvation came to Zacchaeus and his household because he looked to Jesus in faith. He received Him joyfully and called Him "Lord." "Today," Jesus said, "salvation has come to this house, because he also is a son of Abraham; for the Son of Man has come to seek and to save that which was lost" (verses 9, 10).

Jesus accomplished His mission of seeking and saving the lost by being lifted up, just as Moses lifted up the serpent in the wilderness. The prophecy of Jesus was fulfilled: "And I, if I am lifted up from the earth, will draw all peoples to Myself" (John 12:32).

Not everyone will choose to look to Jesus and live. Some will deliberately turn away, and die in their sins. Each one of us has a decision to make, one way or the other, but whoever chooses to look to Jesus in faith will live.

## Prophets and Apostles

God provided testimonies from prophets and apostles regarding the mission of Jesus the Messiah. About 700 years before Jesus was born Isaiah prophesied: "He was wounded for our transgressions, He was bruised for our iniquities; the chastisement for our peace was upon Him, and by His stripes we are healed. All we like sheep have gone astray; we have turned, every one, to his own way; and the Lord has laid on Him the iniquity of us all" (Isaiah 53:5, 6).

John the Baptist pointed at Jesus and declared, "Behold! The Lamb of God who takes away the sin of the world!" (John 1:29). The apostle Peter, an eyewitness of the fulfillment of Isaiah's prophecy, testified: "Who, when He was reviled, did not revile in return; when He suffered, He did not threaten, but committed Himself to Him who judges righteously; who Himself bore our sins in His own body on the tree, that we, having died to sins, might live for righteousness—by whose stripes you were healed" (1 Peter 2:23, 24).

Once Saul of Tarsus was fully convinced Jesus was the Christ, it transformed his own life, and he wrote these words to the followers of Jesus in Rome: "God demonstrates His own love toward us, in that while we were still sinners, Christ died for us" (Romans 5:8). Saul, later called the apostle Paul, knew what he was talking about. He had been an enemy of Jesus, persecuting His followers. In a letter to Timothy he wrote, "This is a faithful saying and worthy of all acceptance, that Christ Jesus came into the world to save sinners, of whom I am chief" (1 Timothy 1:15).

That's why the apostle rejoiced when he wrote these words to the Christians in Rome: "If you confess with your mouth the

Lord Jesus and believe in your heart that God has raised Him from the dead, you will be saved. For with the heart one believes unto righteousness, and with the mouth confession is made unto salvation. For the Scripture says, 'Whoever believes on Him will not be put to shame.' For there is no distinction between Jew and Greek, for the same Lord over all is rich to all who call upon Him. For 'whoever calls on the name of the Lord shall be saved'" (Romans 10:9-13).

## Baptism and the Gift

How do we publicly demonstrate our acceptance of Jesus as our personal Savior? The answer is very clear both in the teachings and in the example of Jesus. Jesus said, "He who believes and is baptized will be saved" (Mark 16:16), and "Go therefore and make disciples of all the nations, baptizing them in the name of the Father and of the Son and of the Holy Spirit" (Matthew 28:19).

Baptism is both a confession of our sin and an acknowledgment that we have accepted Jesus as our Savior. When Jesus came to be baptized by John the Baptist in the river Jordan, John tried to prevent Him by saying, "I need to be baptized by You, and are You coming to me?" (Matthew 3:14). Jesus had no sin to confess and thus did not require a Savior. John was right about that, but notice Jesus' response: "Permit it to be so now, for thus it is fitting for us to fulfill all righteousness" (verse 15).

Jesus set an example for all those who would follow in His

steps. That's why Peter preached on the day of Pentecost, "Repent, and let every one of you be baptized in the name of Jesus Christ for the remission of sins" (Acts 2:38).

God has a special gift for each person baptized as a confession of Jesus as Savior. Look again at Acts 2:38. "Repent, and let every one of you be baptized in the name of Jesus Christ for the remission of sins; and you shall receive the *gift* of the Holy Spirit."

That's exactly what happened to Jesus at His baptism. "When He had been baptized, Jesus came up immediately from the water; and behold, the heavens were opened to Him, and He saw the Spirit of God descending like a dove and alighting upon Him. And suddenly a voice came from heaven, saying, 'This is My beloved Son, in whom I am well pleased'" (Matthew 3:16, 17).

God did not send His Son into the world to condemn the world, but to save it through Him. The Lord so loves the world—and that includes *you*—that He gave His only begotten Son that whoever believes in Him should not perish, but have everlasting life.

So let the cry go out throughout the camp. Let the cry go out throughout the church. Let the cry go out throughout your city. Let the cry go out throughout the world. Not as a wail of death, but a proclamation of life. Jesus, the Son of man, has come to seek and to save that which was lost. Look to Jesus in faith, and live.

# 4

## What Jesus Taught About His Return

Our family has moved from one house to another more times than any of us would like to remember. We all agree that it is an incredible amount of work. However, one of the benefits of moving is that you sometimes rediscover precious treasures—things that have been lost for years are found.

My wife and I came across one such treasure while packing for a move a few years ago. It happened to be on a cassette tape. I know that doesn't sound like much—especially since cassette tapes are now obsolete. Yet to our family that cassette tape was worth its weight in gold. That's because it was a recording of our two sons, Christopher and Jonathan, when they were young boys. They were singing a song that Christopher had learned in kindergarten. Here are the words to the song:

"One day I'll look up and see Jesus coming down for me,

   Sitting on a cloud so white with His holy angels bright.

   O then, I will shout and sing, 'Glory! Glory! Glory!'

   He has come, our heavenly King, 'Glory! Glory! Glory!'"

Whether our sons realized it or not, they were sharing the radical teaching of Jesus regarding His return in glory. The second coming of Jesus is one of the most precious truths of the whole Bible. This radical teaching of Jesus causes many people to say, "Glory! Glory! Glory!" Yet it also challenges a lot of strange ideas that people have about His return—how He will arrive back at this earth, what it will be like, or whether He'll even come at all. As we consider the radical teaching of Jesus about His return, I have divided it into three parts: the good news, the bad news, and the most important news.

## The Good News

First, the good news: The return of Jesus in glory is *certain*. This is something worth remembering. When Jesus spoke to His disciples in the upper room, He said, "Let not your heart be troubled; you believe in God, believe also in Me. In My Father's house are many mansions; if it were not so, I would have told you. I go to prepare a place for you. And if I go and prepare a place for you, *I will come again* and receive you to Myself; that where I am, there you may be also" (John 14:1–3, emphasis supplied). The Greek verb translated "I will come" might literally be rendered "I *am* coming again." The futuristic present tense implies that His return is as certain as if it were *already happening*!

In another conversation with His disciples, just days before His crucifixion, Jesus said, "For as the lightning comes from the east and flashes to the west, so also *will* the coming of the Son of Man be" (Matthew 24:27). The glorious return of Jesus, like lightning streaking across the sky, *will* happen. His second coming is without question.

"Then the sign of the Son of Man *will appear* in heaven, and then all the tribes of the earth will mourn, and they *will see* the Son of Man coming on the clouds of heaven with power and great glory" (Matthew 24:30). The return of Jesus is certain, and it will be highly visible—like lightning across a dark sky. The apostle John reinforces this truth: "Behold, He is coming with clouds, and every eye will see Him" (Revelation 1:7).

Jesus gave the apostle Paul a special revelation regarding His second advent, recorded in 1 Thessalonians 4:15-17: "For this we say to you by the word of the Lord, that we who are alive and remain until the coming of the Lord will by no means precede those who are asleep. For the Lord Himself will descend from heaven with a shout, with the voice of an archangel, and with the trumpet of God. And the dead in Christ will rise first. Then we who are alive and remain shall be caught up together with them in the clouds to meet the

Lord in the air. And thus we shall always be with the Lord."

Because His return is certain, Jesus counseled His followers: "Therefore you also be ready, for the Son of Man *is coming* at an hour you do not expect" (Matthew 24:44). There is nothing tentative about the radical teaching of Jesus regarding His return. His visible, audible, and dramatic second advent is certain. The Son of man *is coming,* and that's good news.

For several years my wife worked as a nurse practitioner in an ob-gyn practice. During that time she interacted with a lot of pregnant women, most of whom didn't know the exact day their babies would be delivered. Some of them didn't even know they were pregnant when they came in for their first checkup. As the weeks and months of the pregnancy progressed, it became more and more evident a baby was on its way. People could see the signs, and they knew that the arrival of the baby was certain.

Jesus tells us, "My return is definite. You can see the signs." We can read about them in Matthew 24:4-13: "Take heed that no one deceives you. For many will come in My name, saying, 'I am the Christ,' and will deceive many. And you will hear of wars and rumors of wars. See that you are not troubled; for all these things must come to pass, but the end is not yet. For nation will rise against nation, and kingdom against kingdom. And there will be famines, pestilences, and earthquakes in various places. All these are the beginning of sorrows.

Then they will deliver you up to tribulation and kill you, and you will be hated by all nations for My name's sake. And then many will be offended, will betray one another, and will hate one another. Then many false prophets will rise up and deceive many. And because lawlessness will abound, the love of many will grow cold. But he who endures to the end shall be saved." The final sign that Jesus mentions that points to His return is already being fulfilled. "And this gospel of the kingdom will be preached in all the world as a witness to all nations, and then the end will come" (verse 14).

According to Jesus, while no one knows the day or the hour of His return, we can recognize that it is approaching. That, my friend, is good news.

## The Bad News

But we also have to consider some bad news that Jesus taught regarding His second coming. Many of the professed followers of Jesus *will not be ready* for it. Jesus presented a parable about a wedding to illustrate this. "Then the kingdom of heaven shall be likened to ten virgins who took their lamps and went out to meet the bridegroom. Now five of them were wise, and five were foolish. Those who were foolish took their lamps and took no oil with them, but the wise took oil in their vessels with their lamps" (Matthew 25:1-4).

This wedding represents the certain return of Jesus. All 10 virgins were waiting for the arrival of the bridegroom, had lamps, and had oil in their lamps. Thus all of them had, at some point, received the anointing of God's Spirit.

"But while the bridegroom was delayed, they all slumbered and slept. And at midnight a cry was heard: 'Behold, the bridegroom is coming; go out to meet him!' Then all those virgins arose and trimmed their lamps. And the foolish said to the wise, 'Give us some of your oil, for our lamps are going out.' But the wise answered, saying, 'No, lest there should not be enough for us and you; but go rather to those who sell, and buy for yourselves.' And while they went to buy, the bridegroom came, and those who were ready went in with him to the wedding; and the door was shut. Afterward the other virgins came also, saying, 'Lord, Lord, open to us!' But he answered and said, 'Assuredly, I say to you, I do not know you.' Watch therefore, for you know neither the day nor the hour in which the Son of Man is coming" (verses 5-13).

In Jesus' parable 50 percent of the professed followers of Jesus were *not ready* for His return. Then in the parable that follows—that of the talents—33 percent of the servants were *not ready*. While I don't think Jesus was trying to give us a true, measurable percentage, one lesson is startlingly clear: not all who profess to be followers of Jesus will be prepared for the Second Advent. That, my friend, is bad news.

I heard a story some time ago about three men standing with some suitcases on the platform of a train station. They were so engrossed in conversation that they seemed oblivious to anything happening around them. After a few minutes the train pulled into the station. Passengers disembarked. New passengers boarded the train. But none of the three men seemed to notice. They simply continued their intense conversation. Finally the whistle blew, and the train began to move. Immediately a flurry of activity erupted on the platform. Two of the men grabbed suitcases and began running toward the train. The train started picking up speed. Both men ran as fast as they could, tossed the suitcases in through an open door, and barely managed to jump on board as the train left the station.

The third man, who had remained motionless on the platform, stared at the departing train, then suddenly burst into laughter. The stationmaster, who had observed the whole situation, couldn't contain his curiosity. Walking over to the laughing stranger, he said, "Sir, I'm puzzled. I saw your two companions run for the train and barely get on board before the train pulled out of the station. Then I noticed you standing here, and all of a sudden you started laughing. I just don't understand. What's so funny?" Composing himself, the man looked at the stationmaster and said, "I can understand that the situation didn't look very humorous to you, sir. But you see, those two men came to say goodbye to *me*. *I* was the one who was supposed to get on the train!"

Those three men became so distracted that in the end none of them ended up in the right place. Two men caught a train they weren't supposed to ride, and the intended traveler was still standing on the platform. The story generally makes people smile, but I think you would agree it's no laughing matter to think about people not being ready for the return of Jesus. Not when it could be someone you love who might "miss the train." I think it would be a tragedy for *anyone* to be left "standing on the platform" when Jesus arrives. Yet many of those who call Jesus "Lord" *will* miss the train. This is bad news indeed.

## The Most Important News

We've seen that Jesus taught that His return is certain, but that not all who claim His name will be ready for the event. So what's the most important news Jesus presented about His return? That Jesus wants *you* to be ready . . . that He wants *all of us* to be ready. We find this radical teaching in the same portion of Scripture, beginning with Matthew 24:36: "But of that day and hour no one knows, not even the angels of heaven, but My Father only." Notice that the question is not *whether* Jesus will return, but *when*. To this question Jesus gave the following response: "Only the Father knows."

"But as the days of Noah were, so also will the coming of the Son of Man be. For as in the days before the flood, they were eating and drinking, marrying and giving in marriage, until the day that Noah entered the ark, and did not know until the flood came and took them all away, so also will the coming of the Son of Man be. Then two men will be in the field: one will be taken and the other left. Two women will be grinding at the mill: one will be taken and the other left. Watch therefore, for you do not know what hour your Lord is coming" (Matthew 24:37-42).

Many people wonder about this passage. Some claim that there will be a time when those who are righteous will be "raptured" to heaven, leaving many behind to have a second chance to make their decision to follow Christ. Yet this idea is a dangerous deception. It could tempt one to say, "I'll just wait for the really good people to be taken, and then I'll get my life together so that I can be saved, too." However, if we closely examine the radical teaching of Jesus about His return, we will discover that a secret rapture of the saints, giving others a second chance for salvation, is *not* what He said would happen.

Jesus compared the time of His coming to the days of Noah. For 120 years Noah had warned the people living at the time of the Flood yet they were still surprised by it. They continued on with normal living until the day Noah entered the ark, and *did not know* until the Flood arrived and *took them all away.* It is clear from this radical teaching that those who were "taken away" were those who were *not* ready—those who perished.

The picture gets even clearer when we look at the parallel passage in the Gospel of Luke. "And as it was in the days of

Noah, so it will be also in the days of the Son of Man: They ate, they drank, they married wives, they were given in marriage, until the day that Noah entered the ark, and the flood came and *destroyed them all*. Likewise as it was also in the days of Lot: They ate, they drank, they bought, they sold, they planted, they built; but on the day that Lot went out of Sodom it rained fire and brimstone from heaven and *destroyed them all*" (Luke 17:26-29). There exists no second chance for those who are left behind. They are destroyed, just as it happened with those of both Noah's and Lot's generations. Only a few were *left* and saved, while all the rest were *taken away* and destroyed.

Yet the whole point of Jesus' teaching of His return in Matthew 24 appears in verse 44: "Therefore you also *be ready*." He *is* coming. The return of Jesus is *certain*. Although the time is unknown, the most important news is this: Jesus wants you to be ready.

## Wildfires

When we lived in the mountains of southern California, we became accustomed to the wildfires that occur during the dry summer months. One summer a wildfire came within a half mile of our house. It was a fascinating sight. The fire swept up the south side of the ridge, right over the top, and was on its way down to where we lived. The firefighters were well prepared, with their fire trucks strategically positioned. Air support came in the form of small twin-engine planes, helicopters, and a huge plane that dropped fire retardant.

While I stood outside gawking at the pyrotechnic display, my wife was busy in the house. Gathering up all our important papers, she carried out 15-20 family photo albums and put them in the trunk of the car. Then she packed a change of clothes for everyone. While I was sightseeing, my wife was preparing. I was preoccupied. But she was ready.

It is so easy to be preoccupied with unimportant things. Pyrotechnic displays, flashing lights, and helicopter stunts capture our attention and distract us from essential daily preparation for the return of Jesus. I think most people really want to be ready. Yet we've read that many of Jesus' professed followers will *not.* So how do we go about *being* ready?

We find the answer in the parable of the 10 virgins. To those who were not prepared, Jesus said, "I do not know you" (Matthew 25:12). If those who don't know Jesus are *not* ready, then the way to *be* ready is to *know* Jesus. That is why He prayed: "And this is eternal life, that they may know You, the only true God, and Jesus Christ whom You have sent" (John 17:3). Life is found in knowing Jesus. "God has given us eternal life, and this life is in His Son. He who has the Son has life" (1 John 5:11, 12).

If you want to follow the counsel of Jesus to *be ready*, then you need to make sure that you know Him and that He knows you. The wise virgins maintained the relationship, keeping a "steady flame in the lamp." The foolish virgins had an experience of knowing God in the past, but they allowed the flame of the relationship to be extinguished. So if I am going to *be ready* today, then I need to know Jesus *today* and every day as I wait for His certain return.

Of course, this leads to the question: How can I know that I have a right relationship with Jesus? Is there a way to be sure? The answer is yes. Jesus said, "Not everyone who says to Me, 'Lord, Lord,' shall enter the kingdom of heaven, but he who does the will of My Father in heaven" (Matthew 7:21). A healthy relationship with Jesus will manifest itself in loving obedience to His commands.

It is easy to misinterpret this teaching of Jesus. He is not saying that the works we do will save us. If that were the case, none of us could have hope. Put very simply, if you have Jesus, you have life, and when you have Jesus, you will do the things He says *because you love Him*.

A relationship with Jesus Christ is a life-changing experience. If you have received Jesus Christ as your personal Savior and Lord, you have everlasting life. You *are ready* for His certain return. That's the most important news of all, because Jesus *wants* you to be ready. He longs for you to experience what's spoken of in the rest of the song that my son Christopher learned so long ago:

"Gabriel will his trumpet blow, wake the sleeping ones below.

They in beauty shall arise to see Jesus in the skies.

O then, I will shout and sing, 'Glory! Glory! Glory!'

He has come, our heavenly King. 'Glory! Glory! Glory!'"

Jesus wants *you* to be ready for that day! He desires for you to join in the chorus that shouts, "Glory! Glory! Glory!" If you want to be ready on *that day*, then be ready *today*. Trust Jesus our Savior today.

# 5

## What Jesus Thought About the Sabbath

How would you respond if I were to tell you, "I decided to do away with the sixth commandment"?

"That's ridiculous!" you might reply. "You can't just do away with one of the Ten Commandments."

What if I told you I was part of a large and influential group of people who had actually made that decision? You'd most likely protest, "That doesn't make any difference. No person, or group of people, has the authority to change God's commandments."

You would be absolutely correct, and Jesus would agree with you. He always honored the commandments of God. He said, "I have kept my Father's commandments and abide in His love" (John 15:10). Jesus also gave this rebuke to the religious leaders of His day: "Why do you also transgress the commandment of God because of your tradition?" (Matthew 15:3).

I'm sure Jesus would say much the same thing today to those who seek to discard any commandment of God and replace it with human ideas or tradition.

## The Ten Commandments

God prefaces the Ten Commandments with these words: "I am the Lord your God, who brought you out of the land of Egypt, out of the house of bondage" (Exodus 20:2).

- "You shall have no other gods before Me" (verse 3).
- "You shall not make for yourself a carved image—any likeness of anything that is in heaven above, or that is in the earth beneath, or that is in the water under the earth; you shall not bow down to them nor serve them. For I, the Lord your God, am a jealous God, visiting the iniquity of the fathers upon the children to the third and fourth generations of those who hate Me, but showing mercy to thousands, to those who love Me and keep My commandments" (verses 4-6).
- "You shall not take the name of the Lord your God in vain, for the Lord will not hold him guiltless who takes His name in vain" (verse 7).
- "Remember the Sabbath day, to keep it holy. Six days you shall labor and do all your work, but the seventh day is the Sabbath of the Lord your God. In it you shall do no work: you, nor your son, nor your daughter, nor your male servant, nor your female servant, nor your cattle,

nor your stranger who is within your gates. For in six days the Lord made the heavens and the earth, the sea, and all that is in them, and rested the seventh day. Therefore the Lord blessed the Sabbath day and hallowed it" (verses 8-11).

- "Honor your father and your mother, that your days may be long upon the land which the Lord your God is giving you" (verse 12).
- "You shall not murder" (verse 13).
- "You shall not commit adultery" (verse 14).
- "You shall not steal" (verse 15).
- "You shall not bear false witness against your neighbor" (verse 16).
- "You shall not covet your neighbor's house, you shall not covet your neighbor's wife, nor his male servant, nor his female servant, nor his ox, nor his donkey, nor anything that is your neighbor's" (verse 17).

I'm certain that God wants us to honor all 10 commandments, but it's interesting to me that only one of them begins with the word "remember." *"Remember* the Sabbath day, to keep it holy" (verse 8). Could it be God knew that someone or some group would claim to have the authority to do away with one of the commandments? Many Christians say the Sabbath doesn't have to be remembered anymore. They say the Sabbath commandment no longer applies to New Testament Christians. I believe many of them are sincere. And they raise two questions about the Sabbath I think we should examine.

## Two Questions

The first question involves the instructions that Jesus gave to His disciples. Some point out that after His resurrection, Jesus never specifically directed them to continue to observe the seventh day of the week as the Sabbath. On the other hand, it can also be said that after His resurrection Jesus never instructed His disciples to *stop* observing the Sabbath, either. So, basing our acceptance or rejection of the Sabbath on what Jesus *didn't* say doesn't seem like a very solid platform to stand on.

The second question arises from an incident in which Jesus quoted from the commandments. In a previous chapter we looked at the story of the rich young ruler recorded in Luke 18:18–23. Some point out that in His conversation with the wealthy young ruler Jesus failed to quote the fourth commandment along with the others. Therefore, they infer, it is no longer necessary to "remember" the Sabbath. As part of His conversation with the Jewish leader Jesus said, "You know the commandments: 'Do not commit adultery,' 'Do not murder,' 'Do not steal,' 'Do not bear false witness,' 'Honor your father and your mother'" (verse 20).

Jesus quoted the seventh, the sixth, the eighth, the ninth, and the fifth commandments, in that order. Can this text be used to prove that Jesus no longer expected New Testament Christians to remember the Sabbath day, to honor it? Hardly. While it's true Jesus doesn't quote the fourth commandment, neither does He quote:

- the first commandment: "You shall have no other gods before Me."
- the second commandment: "You shall not make for yourself a carved image."
- the third commandment: "You shall not take the name of the LORD your God in vain."
- the tenth commandment: "You shall not covet."

If we work on the logic that only the ones Jesus quoted are still binding, we would also have to do away with the other commandments Jesus omitted. Would it be sound logic to argue that none of those commandments are binding either? On the contrary, Jesus Himself said, "Do not think that I came to destroy the Law or the Prophets. I did not come to destroy but to fulfill" (Matthew 5:17). So the question is, then, what would Jesus want us to know about the commandment that begins with the word "remember," and how did He relate to it in His life?

## Jesus and the Sabbath

What *did* Jesus teach about the Sabbath? We can have no doubt Jesus honored the Sabbath during His earthly life. Luke recorded, "As His custom was, He went into the synagogue on the Sabbath day, and stood up to read" (Luke 4:16). Jesus *remembered* the fourth commandment Sabbath regularly. It was His normal habit to go to the synagogue on the Sabbath day. He also expected His followers to remember the Sabbath day. He made that clear when He prophesied the destruction of Jerusalem: "And pray that your flight may not be in winter or on the Sabbath" (Matthew 24:20).

In fact, Jesus sought to help people understand the true meaning of the Sabbath. The religious leaders of His day had mutilated the Sabbath by surrounding it with a myriad of man-made rules and regulations. Under those rules the Sabbath had become a burden to the people, and Jesus longed for them to rediscover the true significance of God's holy day. His radical teaching about the Sabbath also challenges us to discover the true meaning of this great commandment of God.

## Sabbath Made for Man

I have no doubt the Jewish leaders of Jesus' day had good intentions when they made all the extra rules and regulations on how to observe the Sabbath. They wanted to make certain that it was honored properly. But instead of preserving the Sabbath, they turned it into something God never intended it to be. They transformed God's holy day into a burden, and when they saw the disciples of Jesus plucking heads of grain as they walked through a field on the Sabbath, the Pharisees basically said, "They are breaking the Sabbath. That's not allowed! According to our human-made supplements to the fourth commandment, that's a transgression."

Jesus responded, "The Sabbath was made for man, and not man for the Sabbath" (Mark 2:27). He could speak with authority because He was "Lord of the Sabbath" (verse 28). The apostle John tells us, speaking by the Holy Spirit, that all things were made by the Word, the same Word who became flesh and dwelt among us (John 1:3, 14). The eternal Son of God, the Word who came in flesh as Jesus of Nazareth, was the one who created the Sabbath as the concluding act of His creative work. "Thus the heavens and the earth, and all the host of them, were finished. And on the seventh day God ended His work which He had done, and He rested on the seventh day from all His work which He had done. Then God blessed the seventh day and sanctified it, because in it He rested from all His work which God had created and made" (Genesis 2:1-3).

The Son of God created the Sabbath, blessed it, and sanctified it. That's why He could claim, "Therefore the Son of Man is also Lord of the Sabbath" (Mark 2:28). According to Jesus Himself, He created the Sabbath for humanity. God intends it to be a time of *blessing*, not a burden.

For six days we do our work, and if it were not for the blessing of the Sabbath, many of us would probably labor seven days a week. We *need* the Sabbath. It is not an additional obligation that complicates our already hectic lives—it's a blessing! And for a number of reasons:

- We need the Sabbath as a time of blessing to remember who we are and who God is.
- We need the Sabbath to remember that our lives are more than cosmic coincidences.
- We need the Sabbath to remember that there is more to our present than making a living.
- We need the Sabbath to remember that there is more to our future than retirement.

The Sabbath is not only a time of blessing for us as individuals. It is also a time of blessing as we allow God to bless others through us. Jesus said, "It is lawful to do good on the Sabbath" (Matthew 12:12). That seems like a strange comment until you realize that the Pharisees even saw works of kindness and mercy on the Sabbath as a transgression of the Sabbath commandment. But Jesus said, "No, the Sabbath was made for humanity—it is *lawful* to do good on the Sabbath." If you see someone in need, there is no better time to let God bless that person through you than on the Sabbath day.

### Blessing My Neighbor

I remember one Sabbath when I returned home from church to our house in Wescosville, Pennsylvania, and saw my neighbor Michael Henry standing in front of his car, bending over the open engine compartment. That's usually a sign there's a problem. If the car isn't working, people look under the hood even if they have no idea what they're searching for!

So I called out to him, "What's the problem, Mike?"

"Oh," he said, "it's my battery. It's dead!" I stopped my car, went into my garage, got my jumper cables, slid back behind the steering wheel, and drove over into his driveway. Within a few minutes, we had hooked up the jumper cables, and his car was running.

As I waved goodbye, he said, "I really appreciate your help. I wasn't going to ask you for assistance because I know it's your Sabbath." I appreciated his sensitivity. If he had asked me to remodel his bathroom, I'd have suggested rescheduling. But he was in trouble. He needed help, and I was happy to lend a hand because the Sabbath is a time of blessing. Not only is it an occasion when we *are* blessed; it's also one when we can extend blessing to those around us. So bless someone each Sabbath day. Visit people in the hospital. Invite someone who is lonely to take a walk with your family. Share your lunch with someone, and do so knowing that you are experiencing the true meaning of the Sabbath. It is a time of blessing, just as Jesus taught.

## Overturning the Traditions

Jesus taught that the Sabbath is not only an opportunity for blessing but also a time for healing. As we read the gospel record, we discover that Jesus intentionally healed people on the Sabbath day. He knew His actions would arouse opposition from the religious leaders and that they would accuse Him of being a Sabbathbreaker. Although He could have waited until another day, Jesus could not allow the truth about the Sabbath to continue to be distorted by human traditions. He wanted people to know that the Sabbath is both a day of blessing *and* a day for healing.

## Man at the Pool of Bethesda

The apostle John records a story of a healing on the Sabbath: "After this there was a feast of the Jews, and Jesus went up to Jerusalem. Now there is in Jerusalem by the Sheep Gate a pool, which is called in Hebrew, Bethesda, having five porches. In these lay a great multitude of sick people, blind, lame, paralyzed, waiting for the moving of the water. For an angel went down at a certain time into the pool and stirred up the water; then whoever stepped in first, after the stirring of the water, was made well of whatever disease he had. Now a certain man was there who had an infirmity thirty-eight years. When Jesus saw him lying there, and knew that he already had been in that condition a long time, He said to him, 'Do you want to be made well?' The sick man answered Him, 'Sir, I have no man to put me into the pool when the water is stirred up; but while I am coming, another steps down before me.' Jesus said to him, 'Rise, take up your bed and walk.' And immediately the man was made well, took up his bed, and walked. And that day was the Sabbath" (John 5:1-9).

Why do you think Jesus asked the man to take his sleeping

mat with him? Can you imagine what that mat smelled like? I probably would have said, "Just get up and walk. Forget about the sleeping mat." But Jesus said, "Rise, take up your bed and walk." Again, why do you think Jesus gave those instructions?

We find the answer in John 5:9: "That day was the Sabbath." Jesus deliberately drew attention to the healing. He knew the religious leaders would criticize Him, and it came almost immediately. "The Jews therefore said to him who was cured, 'It is the Sabbath; it is not lawful for you to carry your bed'" (verse 10). They totally missed the opportunity to praise the name of the Lord. This man had been a paralytic for 38 years, and now he had been made whole, but the religious leaders were completely oblivious to that fact. All they could see was a transgression of their Sabbath regulations.

Jesus performed His miracle in spite of their opposition. He healed the man on the Sabbath day despite the criticism He would receive. Why? Because the Sabbath is a time for healing. Jesus could not tolerate a distorted view of the Sabbath. God had given the Sabbath as a blessing, not a burden.

## A Crippled Woman

Let's consider a second miracle Jesus intentionally performed on the Sabbath. The story appears in Luke 13:10-17.

"Now He was teaching in one of the synagogues on the Sabbath. And behold, there was a woman who had a spirit of infirmity eighteen years, and was bent over and could in no way raise herself up. But when Jesus saw her, He called her to Him and said to her, 'Woman, you are loosed from your infirmity.' And He laid His hands on her, and immediately she was made straight, and glorified God. But the ruler of the synagogue answered with indignation, because Jesus had healed on the Sabbath; and he said to the crowd, 'There are six days on which men ought to work; therefore come and be healed on them, and not on the Sabbath day.' The Lord then answered him and said, 'Hypocrite! Does not each one of you on the Sabbath loose his ox or donkey from the stall, and lead it away to water it? So ought not this woman, being a daughter of Abraham, whom Satan has bound—think of it—for eighteen years, be loosed from this bond on the Sabbath?' And when He said these things, all His adversaries were put to shame; and all the multitude rejoiced for all the glorious things that were done by Him."

We learn from this example of Jesus that it is not only lawful to do good on the Sabbath; it is also lawful to heal on the Sabbath. In fact, the Sabbath is a time when healing *ought* to occur. There's no better occasion than the Sabbath to be made whole. That's a radical teaching of Jesus.

## Man With a Withered Hand

Another Sabbath Jesus entered a synagogue and noticed a man who had a withered hand. The story is recorded in the

Gospel of Mark. If you read between the lines, it looks like a setup. The religious leaders had actually placed this man in the congregation as a trap for Jesus. "So they watched Him closely, whether He would heal him on the Sabbath, so that they might accuse Him. And He said to the man who had the withered hand, 'Step forward.' Then He said to them, 'Is it lawful on the Sabbath to do good or to do evil, to save life or to kill?' But they kept silent. And when He had looked around at them with anger, being grieved by the hardness of their hearts, He said to the man, 'Stretch out your hand.' And he stretched it out, and his hand was restored as whole as the other. Then the Pharisees went out and immediately plotted with the Herodians against Him, how they might destroy Him" (Mark 3:2-6).

Oblivious to the true meaning of the Sabbath, these religious leaders were so caught up in their human-made regulations that they plotted against the Son of God, first to catch Him transgressing their distorted view of the Sabbath, and then to *kill* Him for doing so. No wonder Jesus was "grieved by the hardness of their hearts."

What a tragedy! But it's also a tragedy if *we* miss the true meaning of the Sabbath. We could fall into the trap of keeping the Sabbath holy just because "it's the right thing to do," just to fulfill some legalistic obligation. Or we could fail to remember the Sabbath at all, believing the human tradition that we no longer need to observe the Sabbath.

The radical teaching of Jesus about the Sabbath is clear. Sabbath is a time of blessing and healing. Then why have so many people—even Christians—forgotten the very day that God told us to "remember"? We find a clue in these words of Jesus about Satan's deceptive activity: "He was a murderer from the beginning, and does not stand in the truth, because there is no truth in him. When he speaks a lie, he speaks from his own resources, for he is a liar and the father of it" (John 8:44).

## Lies in the Garden

What lies did Satan tell our first parents in the Garden of Eden? He presented at least two. "Now the serpent was more cunning than any beast of the field which the Lord God had made. And he said to the woman, 'Has God indeed said, "You shall not eat of every tree of the garden"?' And the woman said to the serpent, 'We may eat the fruit of the trees of the garden; but of the fruit of the tree which is in the midst of the garden, God has said, "You shall not eat it, nor shall you touch it, lest you die."' Then the serpent said to the woman, 'You will not surely die'" (Genesis 3:1-4).

There's the first lie: "You will not surely die." We'll explore the ramifications of that lie in a later chapter when we consider the radical teaching of Jesus about death. But Genesis 3:5 records a second falsehood: "For God knows that in the day you eat of it your eyes will be opened, and you will be like God, knowing good and evil."

Did you notice Satan's second lie? "You will be like God." According to the prophet Isaiah, that inappropriate desire was Satan's downfall. He wanted to be like God. Isaiah gave this inspired testimony: "How you are fallen from heaven, O Lucifer, son of the morning! How you are cut down to the ground, you who weakened the nations! For you have said in your heart: 'I will ascend into heaven, I will exalt my throne above the stars of God; I will also sit on the mount of the congregation on the farthest sides of the north; I will ascend above the heights of the clouds, I will be like the Most High'" (Isaiah 14:12-14).

Satan's temptation to the first family was for them to be like God. He wanted to convince them that they could assume divine power and authority. So it makes sense that the one commandment he would particularly want us to forget is the one that talks about God our *Creator*. The Sabbath is a weekly reminder that we *aren't* God. We didn't create ourselves. Neither are we the result of some cosmic accident. Hear again the appeal of our Creator: "Remember the Sabbath day, to keep it holy. Six days you shall labor and do all your work, but the seventh day is the Sabbath of the Lord your God. . . . For in six days the Lord made the heavens and the earth, the sea, and all that is in them, and rested the seventh day. Therefore the Lord blessed the Sabbath day and hallowed it" (Exodus 20:8-11).

## The Creator's Gift

The Sabbath is a great gift from our Creator's hand. Jesus

didn't do away with the Sabbath. In fact, He made it. He is Lord of the Sabbath. And He didn't tell His followers to forget the Sabbath. Not a single word in Scripture points to Jesus calling for His followers to abandon the Sabbath. Rather, the radical teaching of Jesus reminds us that the Sabbath is a time of blessing and healing. Followers of Jesus need the Sabbath! It is a precious gift from our Creator and Redeemer to remind us of who we are and who He is.

Do you need blessing and healing in your life today? There is no better time to experience blessing than on the Sabbath day. And there is no better time to experience healing than on the Sabbath day, because the Sabbath is a divinely ordained day of blessing and healing.

That's why it's good for us to gather together for worship every Sabbath. Yes, we could worship God by ourselves. We could go to the mountains or the desert and spend time alone with Him, remembering who we are and who He is, and sometimes that is meaningful and appropriate. But it's also good for us to assemble on the Sabbath day, because as we worship together, we can experience blessing and healing as a community.

- We can experience blessing as we fellowship together.
- We can experience blessing as we bear one another's burdens.
- We can experience healing from our stresses and anxieties as we cast all our worries and concerns upon God, because He cares for us.

- We can experience healing from our sense of loneliness and alienation as we gather together in Jesus' name.
- We can experience healing for our emotions and our bodies as we come in faith and claim divine promises.

Yes, the Sabbath is a time of blessing and healing. Our Creator told us to *remember* the Sabbath day because He loves us. He wants to bless us and to heal us. That's the radical teaching of Jesus.

# 6

## What Jesus Taught About the Judgment

When I was 12 years old, I had to stand before a judge, and I can still remember how terrified I was. My knees knocked together, sweat trickled down my back, and I had a terrible sense of impending doom. And I hadn't even done anything wrong! I had been summoned to court simply because someone had stolen *my* bicycle from the parking lot of the local swimming pool.

But I remember how small I felt, with the judge sitting way up above me behind a huge wooden bench. To me, he looked like a massive eagle perched up in a tree, ready to swoop down. Close to his right hand rested a wooden gavel that I imagined he might use to strike me on the head. I'm sure it wasn't there for that purpose, but it was scary nonetheless. All in all, it was a most traumatic experience for me.

Many of us grew up with ideas about the final judgment that echo my experience in court. We think about the judgment with anxiety and fear, and imagine God with a giant gavel just waiting to strike us down for our sins. Perhaps we have heard the messages of the three angels, which begin with the words: "Fear God and give glory to Him, for the hour of His judgment has come" (Revelation 14:7). Or we may have read the solemn warning of the apostle Paul that "we must all appear before the judgment seat of Christ, that each one may receive the things done in the body, according to what he has done, whether good or bad" (2 Corinthians 5:10). It all sounds very disturbing, doesn't it?

In this chapter we will examine the radical teaching of Jesus about the judgment. You may be pleasantly surprised to discover that what He taught is actually good news indeed.

## A Day of Judgment

The teaching of Jesus clearly indicates that there will be a day of judgment. "Woe to you, Chorazin! Woe to you, Bethsaida! For if the mighty works which were done in you had been done in Tyre and Sidon, they would have repented long ago in sackcloth and ashes. But I say to you, it will be more tolerable for Tyre and Sidon in the day of judgment than for you. And you, Capernaum, who are exalted to heaven, will be brought down to Hades; for if the mighty works which were done in you had been done in Sodom, it would have remained until this day. But I say to you that it shall be more tolerable for the land of Sodom in the day of judgment than for you" (Matthew 11:21-24). Jesus also declared: "For every idle word men may speak, they will give account of it in the day of judgment" (Matthew 12:36).

That doesn't sound very encouraging, does it? Who could ever claim to have never spoken idle words? If we are to give account for every moment of corrupt communication, then we're all in big trouble! So where's the good news?

## Good News

We'll begin our search for the good news Jesus taught about the judgment in the Gospel of John. Jesus said, "For the Father judges *no one*" (John 5:22). Who then is the judge in the final judgment? Jesus continues: "But has committed all judgment to the Son" (verse 22).

The first piece of good news in the radical teaching of Jesus about the judgment is that *He* is the judge. During my anxious encounter with that judge perched up behind the huge wooden desk, do you think I would have reacted differently if I had known him? Do you imagine I would have experienced different emotions if he had been my friend? Would it have helped me feel more relaxed if he had waved at me, winked at me with a sparkle in his eye, and smiled at me? Of course! I wouldn't have been shaking in my shoes if I'd known the judge was my friend who cared for me and loved me.

Jesus says, "There's something very important that I want you to know about the judgment: I'm the judge. I'm in charge! I render the verdicts." That's good news! Our Savior, the Lord Jesus Christ, who loves us and gave Himself for us— *He* is the judge. The Father has committed all judgment to the Son. We can let go of the picture of God with a giant gavel waiting to strike us down. If God were "out to get us," then the Son of God could have stayed in heaven. But instead, God loved the world so much that He *sent* His Son to save us.

The second piece of good news in the radical teaching of Jesus about the judgment is embedded in a story He told about the time when the Son of man will perform His role of judgment. "When the Son of Man comes in His glory, and all the holy angels with Him, then He will sit on the throne of His glory. All the nations will be gathered before Him, and He will separate them one from another, as a shepherd divides his sheep from the goats. And He will set the sheep on His right hand, but the goats on the left. Then the King will say to those on His right hand, 'Come, you blessed of My Father, inherit the kingdom prepared for you from the foundation of the world: for I was hungry and you gave Me food; I was thirsty and you gave Me drink; I was a stranger and you took Me in; I was naked and you clothed Me; I was sick and you visited Me; I was in prison and you came to Me.' Then the righteous will answer Him, saying, 'Lord, when did we see You hungry and feed You, or thirsty and give You drink? When did we see You a stranger and take You in, or naked and clothe You? Or when did we see You sick, or in prison, and come to You?' And the King will answer and say to them, 'Assuredly, I say to you, inasmuch as you did it to one of the least of these My brethren, you did it to Me.' Then He will also say to those on the left hand, 'Depart from Me, you cursed, into the everlasting fire prepared for the devil and his angels: for I was hungry and you gave Me no food; I was thirsty and you gave Me no drink; I was a stranger and you did not take Me in, naked and you did not clothe Me, sick and in prison and you did not visit Me.' Then they also will answer Him, saying, 'Lord, when did we see You hungry or thirsty or a stranger or naked or sick or in prison, and did not minister to You?' Then He will answer them, saying, 'Assuredly, I say to you, inasmuch as you did not do it to one of the least of these, you did not do it to Me.' And these will go away into everlasting punishment, but the righteous into eternal life" (Matthew 25:31-46).

We need to be careful not to read too much into this story. The parable isn't teaching us how to be saved. We already know from chapter 3 that we are saved when we look to Jesus in faith as our Savior and Lord. However, we *can* learn from this story what happens in the final judgment.

## More Good News

Jesus' story of the sheep and the goats teaches us that in

the judgment He will identify those who belong to Him. Jesus *knows* who they are. It's true that those who are His will have certain identifying characteristics, but that's not the *reason* they are His. The good works of the sheep are simply the outward manifestation that they belong to Jesus. In the final judgment, Jesus will identify all those who belong to Him.

Back to my experience with the judge: Can you imagine how I would have felt if that judge had gotten me confused with the juvenile kleptomaniac who stole my bike? It would have been devastating for me. Fortunately, even that earthly judge knew who was who, and I can assure you that Jesus, the righteous heavenly judge, knows who is who as well. Jesus recognizes those who belong to Him.

Imagine that we're standing in a room with 100 dogs in it. Now suppose that your dog is part of that pack. Would you be able to identify which dog belonged to you? Of course you would! But how? Because you know your dog. You recognize what it looks like, and your dog responds to your voice. If you called your dog by name, what would happen? It would come running to you.

Do you get the point? Jesus knows those who belong to Him. I'm so glad that He is the one who oversees the final judgment, aren't you? I don't mean to offend you, but I'm glad you're not the one who identifies those who belong to Jesus. I'm sure you are equally glad that I'm not the one either. Why? Because people look at the outward appearance, but God sees the heart.

If any of us saw the woman crumpled up at the feet of Jesus, we might have told her to go stand with the goats. But Jesus recognized the beaten, bruised, used, and abused woman as a lamb of His flock. If we spotted the crooked tax collector who appeared to have more money than morals, we might have told Zacchaeus to join the goats. But Jesus recognized this undersized wheeler-dealer up in the tree as a lamb of His flock.

And what about the foul-mouthed fisherman who seemed to change his allegiance faster than a quick-change artist? Had it been either of us, we might have herded Peter over to the goats. But Jesus recognized this feisty and flawed firecracker as a lamb of His flock. Aren't you glad that it's Jesus who identifies all those who are His?

With Jesus doing the identifying, our key issue is not *how much* we have done or even *what* we have done, but to *whom* we belong. If we belong to Jesus, our lives *will* bear the fruit of that connection with the Lord of life.

## The Best News

The radical teaching of Jesus about the judgment has yet another piece of good news, and it's the best of all. In fact, it sounds too good to be true. We find the best news about the judgment in John 5:24. There Jesus addresses not only His hearers on that Sabbath day in Jerusalem but us, as well: "Most assuredly, I say to you, he who hears My word and believes in Him who sent Me has everlasting life."

Now, that is good news! We can know with certainty that through Jesus Christ our Savior and Lord we *have* everlasting life. But Jesus isn't finished. "He who hears My word and believes in Him who sent Me has everlasting life, and shall not come into judgment, but has passed from death into life" (verse 24).

What is the "word" that we need to hear in order to have everlasting life and in order to not come into judgment? Is it a certain word that Jesus spoke, such as "love" or "forgiveness" or "peace"? No. It's not a specific word. Nor is it even a particular combination of words. Jesus gives us the answer in John 6:47: "Most assuredly, I say to you, he who believes in Me has everlasting life."

The Word we need to hear is not a "what" but a "*who*." Jesus is the "Word." We must hear Jesus and believe in the One who sent Him. John tells us that "in the beginning was the Word, and the Word was with God, and the Word was God. He was in the beginning with God. . . . And the Word became flesh and dwelt among us, and we beheld His glory, the glory as of the only begotten of the Father, full of grace and truth" (John 1:1-14). When we hear that Word, when we receive Jesus for who He is—the one who is full of grace and truth, sent from the Father—and believe in the One who sent Him, we have everlasting life, and shall not come into judgment, but have passed from death into life.

The King James Version translates John 5:24 as follows:

"Verily, verily, I say unto you, He that heareth my word, and believeth on him that sent me, hath everlasting life, and shall not come into *condemnation*; but is passed from death unto life." But it's the same Greek word used in John 5:22: "For the Father judgeth no man, but hath committed all *judgment* unto the Son" (KJV). And it's the same Greek word that appears in John 5:26, 27: "For as the Father hath life in himself; so hath he given to the Son to have life in himself; and hath given him authority to execute *judgment* also, because he is the Son of man" (KJV).

The translators of the King James Version may have had difficulty with what Jesus was saying in John 5:24, but to be consistent, since the same Greek word appears in John 5:22, 24, and 27, it should be translated identically in each place. I believe that the New King James Version and many other translations are correct when they render the words of Jesus in John 5:24 as follows: "Most assuredly, I say to you, he who hears My word and believes in Him who sent Me has everlasting life, and shall not come into *judgment*, but has passed from death into life."

## Death to Life

For the person who belongs to Jesus the outcome of the judgment is already settled. It's a done deal. You have *already* passed from death to life!

Do you remember the most difficult exam you ever took in school? I remember mine. It was the year following my encounter with the judge. We had moved from one part of London to another, and I found myself dropped into the physics class at my new school. Unfortunately for me, I hadn't taken physics the previous year, so I was already a year behind when I started the class. I didn't have a clue what was going on. In fact, it seemed like a foreign language to me. Have you ever sat in a class like that? At the end of the year when I took the final exam, I knew I was in trouble. I got 37 percent on the final exam, which, needless to say, was not a passing grade. I crashed and burned! It was a total disaster!

Now, imagine that *you're* back in school, and your teacher comes to you and says, "I've got some bad news and some good news for you. There's going to be a very difficult test next week. In fact, it's so difficult that only one person has ever passed it. That's the bad news." How would that make you feel? Terrified? Anxious? Depressed? But the teacher continues. "Now here's the good news," she says. "I've already taken the test for you, and you made an A!"

Wouldn't that be great news? That's what the final judgment will be like for those who belong to Jesus. Its outcome is already settled. We have already passed from death into life. No longer do we have to be anxious or afraid. Jesus our Savior, who loves us and gave Himself for us, is the judge. He will identify all those who belong to Him, and for all those who are His, the result of the judgment is already settled. That, my friend, is the best news of all!

## Too Good to Be True?

The radical teaching of Jesus about the judgment makes it sound *easy* for those who belong to Jesus. How is it possible for a just and holy God to pass over all of our sins, things worthy of condemnation and death? The prophet Isaiah answered that question about 700 years before the Son of God came to earth. Under the inspiration of the Holy Spirit, Isaiah wrote, "He was wounded for our transgressions, He was bruised for our iniquities; the chastisement for our peace was upon Him, and by His stripes we are healed. All we like sheep have gone astray; we have turned, every one, to his own way; and the Lord has laid on Him the iniquity of us all" (Isaiah 53:5, 6).

When you belong to Jesus, the outcome of the judgment is already settled. It is true that the day of judgment is coming and that we will all have to stand before the judgment seat of Christ. In fact, a careful study of prophecies in the books of Daniel[1] and Revelation[2] reveals that we are already living in the time of the judgment.[3] But we don't need to be anxious or afraid.

Jesus Himself is the judge. No one could possibly be a more loving, more compassionate, more merciful judge than He. Our Savior loved us so much that He gave His own life to save us. Christ ever lives to make intercession for us. Soon He will return in glory that where He is, there we may be also. This same Jesus is the judge! The Father has committed all judgment to the Son, and Jesus knows those who belong to Him.

For them, the outcome of the judgment is already settled. It's a done deal! We don't have to wonder what the outcome will be. Jesus has already told us, "He who hears My word and believes in Him who sent Me has everlasting life, and shall not come into judgment, but has passed from death into life" (John 5:24).

I love the promise of Jesus recorded in John 10:27, 28: "My sheep hear My voice, and I know them, and they follow Me. And I give them eternal life, and they shall never perish; neither shall anyone snatch them out of My hand."

When I was a young pastor in my late 20s, our family lived in Allentown, Pennsylvania. That's where I met Violet Bauman. Violet was a devoted follower of Jesus. She was in her 80s when we became friends. I remember the day I went to the ICU at the hospital to visit her. Her life was slipping away, but she was not afraid. As I took her hand, Violet looked at me and said, "Pastor, the Lord has me in the palm of His hand, and no one can snatch me out!" Knowing that she belonged to Jesus and that He is the judge, she could die in peace and assurance because the outcome of her judgment was already settled.

So let the day of judgment come and Jesus, the righteous judge, take His seat. Let Him identify all those who belong to Him. We do not need to be anxious or afraid. Jesus knows all those who belong to Him and who hear His voice. For those who are His, the outcome of the judgment is already settled. That is good news indeed.

[1] Jesus recognized Daniel as a true prophet of God (see Matthew 24:15).

[2] The apostle John recorded "the Revelation of Jesus Christ, which God gave Him to show His servants—things which must shortly take place" (Revelation 1:1). The book promises a blessing to those who read and hear its words (see verse 3).

[3] For a more detailed study of the prophecies of Daniel and Revelation regarding the final judgment, go to www.TheRadicalTeachingsOfJesus.com.

# 7

## What Jesus Taught About Death

Some years ago my wife and I traveled to Tennessee for a family vacation. Bodil took her faithful suitcase, which we have affectionately named Buford. It's a large suitcase that can hold almost everything needed for a vacation, even if you're planning to stay for several months! When we arrived in Tennessee and prepared to unpack, we encountered one small problem. We had forgotten the key for the suitcase. Buford was locked, and without a chisel or a chain saw, we couldn't get it open. All we needed was one tiny key, but that key was 2,000 miles away!

I had another interesting experience with a key when our youngest son, Jonathan, was just a little boy. We had toured Independence Hall while on vacation in Philadelphia, Pennsylvania. At the conclusion of our tour we visited the gift shop. That's where Jonathan found a very special key—a replica of the original key to the lock on the massive front door of Independence Hall. He was so impressed with it that he bought it, even though it cost $5. After his purchase Jonathan started wondering whether or not it was indeed an exact replica of the original key. So when no one was looking, Jonathan and his daddy sneaked over to the massive front door, quietly slipped the key into the old metal lock, cautiously turned it, and it unlocked! My son was so surprised when it worked that he quickly locked it again! You can imagine how important he felt at that moment. He had "the key" to Independence Hall, the "birthplace of the United States."

The Bible talks about some keys Jesus holds that are much more important than the one to Buford or even the one to Independence Hall. Jesus boldly declares that He has the keys of Hades and of death (Revelation 1:18). Let's begin our study of the radical teaching of Jesus about death by considering the strange story Jesus told about two men—a wealthy landowner and a beggar named Lazarus.

## Rich Man and Lazarus

"There was a certain rich man who was clothed in purple and fine linen and fared sumptuously every day. But there was a certain beggar named Lazarus, full of sores, who was laid at his gate, desiring to be fed with the crumbs which fell from the rich man's table. Moreover the dogs came and licked his sores. So it was that the beggar died, and was carried by the angels to Abraham's bosom. The rich man also died and was buried. And being in torments in Hades, he lifted up his eyes and saw Abraham afar off, and Lazarus in his bosom. Then he cried and said, 'Father Abraham, have mercy on me, and send Lazarus that he may dip the tip of his finger in water and cool my tongue; for I am tormented in this flame.' But Abraham said, 'Son, remember that in your lifetime you received your good things, and likewise Lazarus evil things; but now he is comforted and you are tormented. And besides all this, between us and you there is a great gulf fixed, so that those who want to pass from here to you cannot, nor can those from there pass to us.' Then he said, 'I beg you therefore, father, that you would send him to my father's house, for I have five brothers, that he may testify to them, lest they also come to this place of torment.' Abraham said to him, 'They have Moses and the prophets; let them hear them.' And he said, 'No, father Abraham; but if one goes to them from the dead, they will repent.' But he said to him, 'If they do not hear Moses and the prophets, neither will they be persuaded though one rise from the dead'" (Luke 16:19-31).

During the time of Jesus the Jews recounted numerous fables and legends about imaginary situations. Many scholars suggest this story was a modification of one of those popular fables. But why did Jesus tell it? Was His intention to teach doctrine, to explain the truth about death, or to make some other point using a popular fable of His day? Well, let's look at the tale more closely.

The parable has three main characters: a rich man, a poor beggar named Lazarus, and the patriarch Abraham. The story offers no evidence that the rich man was an unrighteous or ungodly individual. Jesus simply stated that he was rich and lived in luxury. Also we find nothing to indicate that the beggar Lazarus was a godly person who placed his faith in God. Regardless of their character, both men died.

Angels carried the beggar to Abraham's bosom, a popular concept among the Jews in Jesus' time. The rich man ended up in Hades, a Greek word that simply means "the grave." Hades is the equivalent of the Hebrew word "sheol." Here we meet our first problem with taking this story as a literal description of what happens when we die. Nowhere else in the Old Testament or the New Testament is Sheol or Hades described as a place of torment, but this story depicts Hades that way.

What's even more troubling, if we read this fable as a literal description of what happens when we die, is the fact that the realm of the saved (Abraham's bosom) and that of the lost (Hades) are so close to each other that it's possible to see what's happening from one place to the other. People can even talk across the gulf between them. Does that sound like heaven to you? Someplace where you could hear the screams of tormented loved ones for ever and ever?

Jonathan Edwards, a famous early American preacher, proclaimed that the agonies of the damned enhance the bliss of the redeemed. But I don't agree. That makes no sense. I can't imagine that anyone would be happy to see loved ones in pain.

I believe it is a mistake to base any doctrine on this or any other fable. Would it really bring any relief if Lazarus dipped his finger in water, reached across the gulf, and cooled the tongue of this rich man who is in fiery torment? The whole story just doesn't make sense if it's a literal description of what happens when we die. So what *was* the point Jesus was trying to make? I'm convinced that we find the answer in Luke 16:26: "And besides all this, between us and you there is a great gulf fixed, so that those who want to pass from here to you cannot, nor can those from there pass to us."

Once death comes, we have no more opportunity to change. Jesus had just told four other stories about a lost sheep, a lost coin, two lost sons, and an unjust steward who lost his job. Then he related this fable about a lost opportunity. The rich man missed his chance to make wise choices before his life came to an end, and once that happens, any opportunity to change ceases forever. That's a lesson we can learn from the fable of the rich man and Lazarus.

## Another Lazarus

Now, if it's dangerous to build any doctrine about what happens when we die based on this fable, which we obviously cannot take literally, where else in the Gospel record do we find what Jesus taught about death? Let's look at another story, also about a man named Lazarus—but this one is true.

"Now a certain man was sick, Lazarus of Bethany, the town of Mary and her sister Martha. It was that Mary who anointed the Lord with fragrant oil and wiped His feet with her hair, whose brother Lazarus was sick. Therefore the sisters sent to Him, saying, 'Lord, behold, he whom You love is sick'" (John 11:1-3).

Lazarus and his two sisters, Martha and Mary, were friends of Jesus. Whenever He was in the vicinity of Jerusalem, Jesus stayed at their home in Bethany. The disciples probably expected Him to drop whatever He was doing and head straight there in response to the urgent appeal. But He didn't. Instead, the Bible tells us, "When Jesus heard that, He said, 'This sickness is not unto death, but for the glory of God, that the Son of God may be glorified through it.' Now Jesus loved Martha and her sister and Lazarus. So, when He heard that he was sick, He stayed two more days in the place where He was" (verses 4-6).

Finally Jesus left for Bethany, and on the way He shared with His disciples His radical teaching about death. "These things He said, and after that He said to them, 'Our friend Lazarus sleeps, but I go that I may wake him up'" (verse 11). Jesus selected His words very carefully. He knew Lazarus was not taking a nap, but He specifically chose to use the word "sleep" to describe Lazarus' condition in death.

Did the disciples understand what Jesus was saying? No. Notice their reaction: "Then His disciples said, 'Lord, if he sleeps he will get well.' However, Jesus spoke of his death, but they thought that He was speaking about taking rest in sleep. Then Jesus said to them plainly, 'Lazarus is dead'" (verses 12-14).

His followers understood that God would raise the redeemed from the sleep of death. Notice Martha's response to Jesus when He arrived in Bethany: "Jesus said to her, 'Your brother will rise again.' Martha said to Him, 'I know that he will rise again in the resurrection at the last day'" (verses 23, 24).

Undoubtedly, she had heard the radical teaching of Jesus concerning death, recorded in John 5:28, 29. There Jesus says, "Do not marvel at this; for the hour is coming in which all who are in the graves will hear His voice and come forth—those who have done good, to the resurrection of life, and those who have done evil, to the resurrection of condemnation."

Jesus now said to Martha, "I am the resurrection and the life. He who believes in Me, though he may die, he shall live" (John 11:25). Then Martha realized that something out of the ordinary was about to happen. "Then Jesus, again groaning in Himself, came to the tomb. It was a cave, and a stone lay against it. Jesus said, 'Take away the stone.' Martha, the sister of him who was dead, said to Him, 'Lord, by this time there is a stench, for he has been dead four days.' Jesus said to her, 'Did I not say to you that if you would believe you would see the glory of God?' Then they took away the stone from the place where the dead man was lying. And Jesus lifted up His eyes and said, 'Father, I thank You that You have heard Me. And I know that You always hear Me, but because of the people who are standing by I said this, that they may believe that You sent Me'" (John 11:38-42).

Notice carefully what Jesus said next: "Lazarus, come forth!" (verse 43). Jesus didn't use the language of the fable in Luke 16. He didn't say, "Lazarus, come down from Abraham's bosom," even though that was a common Jewish belief regarding what happens to those who die. Nor did He call, "Lazarus, come up from the place of torment in Hades." Instead, He commanded, "Lazarus, come forth!" The Word of God tells us in John 11:44, "He who had died came out bound hand and foot with graveclothes, and his face was wrapped with a cloth. Jesus said to them, 'Loose him, and let him go.'"

## The Silence of Lazarus

Have you noticed that after his special resurrection from the sleep of death Lazarus didn't mention anything about his experience during the previous four days? He didn't announce, "Oh, let me tell you what it was like in Abraham's bosom!" Nor did he exclaim, "Oh, thank You for delivering me from the torment of Hades." Why? Because he was in that rock tomb. That's why Jesus said, "Lazarus, come forth!" Jesus was simply waking Lazarus up from the sleep of death.

So then if Lazarus was in the sleep of death, how did he hear Jesus summon him? The answer is both simple and profound. Lazarus heard Jesus call him in the same way that all who are in the graves will hear the voice of Jesus at the resurrection on the last day. The word of Jesus, the resurrection and the life, is so powerful that in the milliseconds it took for the sound to leave His mouth and travel to the place where Lazarus was lying, a miracle of re-creation occurred.

Lazarus had been dead for *four* days. Martha told Jesus that her brother's body was already stinking. His flesh was rapidly decomposing. But the word of Jesus was so powerful, so full of life, that as soon as He spoke the resurrection began. By the time the words reached Lazarus, his body had already been restored. Awakened from the sleep of death and hearing the words of His Savior, Lazarus obeyed Jesus, as was his habit, and emerged from the tomb.

## Paul's Teaching on Death

The apostle Paul received a special revelation from the risen Christ. Afterward he declared: "But I do not want you to be ignorant, brethren, concerning those who have fallen asleep, lest you sorrow as others who have no hope. For if we believe that Jesus died and rose again, even so God will bring with Him those who sleep in Jesus. For this we say to you *by the word of the Lord,* that we who are alive and remain until the coming of the Lord will by no means precede those who are asleep" (1 Thessalonians 4:13-15). What sleep is Paul talking about here? That of death. He continues: "For the Lord Himself will descend from heaven with a shout, with the voice of an archangel, and with the trumpet of God. And the dead in Christ will rise first" (verse 16).

Paul was restating the radical teaching of Jesus about death. The dead in Christ are asleep, but they will not remain that way forever. They will hear the Savior's voice when He calls, and will awake from the sleep of death in obedience to the Master.

## Jesus Holds the Keys

In the book of Revelation Jesus shared another part of His radical teaching about death. "Do not be afraid; I am the First and the Last. I am He who lives, and was dead, and behold, I am alive forevermore. Amen. And I have the keys of Hades and of death" (Revelation 1:17, 18). We don't need to be afraid of the sleep of death because Jesus has the keys that unlock it! When Jesus died on the cross for our sins and was laid in the garden tomb, Satan thought he had finally won. Jesus was dead. But Satan forgot one very important point. Jesus has the keys to death and its domain, and early Sunday morning He responded to His Father's call. He unlocked death's door and emerged as more than a conqueror. Jesus not only triumphed over death Himself—He conquered it for all who believe in Him.

You do not need to fear death and the grave anymore if you believe in Jesus. Even if you fall asleep in death before our Lord and Savior Jesus Christ returns, you won't stay imprisoned in the tomb forever. Jesus has the keys.

That's why Jesus says, "Whoever lives and believes in me shall never die" (John 11:26). Some of His people may take a rest in the sleep of death, but that's not the end of the story. Jesus says, "I am the resurrection and the life. He who believes in Me, though he may die, he shall live" (verse 25).

Do you believe in Jesus, the Son of God? Have you accepted Him as your personal Savior and Lord? Then for you death has lost its sting, and the grave its victory. For you death is but a sleep, and your Savior holds the keys of Hades—the grave and death.

## What Happens to the Unrepentant?

What about those who don't accept Jesus as their personal Savior? According to the radical teachings of Jesus, what happens to them when they die? Although it isn't pleasant, I have to be honest with you and tell you what Jesus taught: "But whoever causes one of these little ones who believe in Me to stumble, it would be better for him if a millstone were hung around his neck, and he were thrown into the sea. If your hand causes you to sin, cut it off. It is better for you to enter into life maimed, rather than having two hands, to go to hell, into the fire that shall never be quenched. . . . And if your foot causes you to sin, cut it off. It is better for you to enter life lame, rather than having two feet, to be cast into hell, into the fire that shall never be quenched. . . . And if your eye causes you to sin, pluck it out. It is better for you to enter the kingdom of God with one eye, rather than having two eyes, to be cast into hell fire." (Mark 9:42-47).

When are unrepentant sinners cast into that unquenchable fire? When they die? No, not according to Jesus. Jesus taught that death is a sleep for all until the resurrection at the last day, and He foretold *two* resurrections then. "Do not marvel at this; for the hour is coming in which all who are in the graves will hear His voice and come forth—those who have done good, to the resurrection of life, and those who have done evil, to the resurrection of condemnation" (John 5:28, 29).

So what happens to those who have done evil after the resurrection of condemnation? Jesus doesn't tell us here. However, we find the answer in His revelation to His servant John. "The sea gave up the dead who were in it, and Death and Hades delivered up the dead who were in them. And they were judged, each one according to his works. Then Death and Hades were cast into the lake of fire. This is the second death" (Revelation 20:13-15).

What else can we learn about this lake of fire? We find another clue in Revelation 21:7, 8: "He who overcomes shall inherit all things, and I will be his God and he shall be My son. But the cowardly, unbelieving, abominable, murderers, sexually immoral, sorcerers, idolaters, and all liars shall have their part in the lake which burns with fire and brimstone, which is the second death."

We don't know for sure how long the fire burns, but the result is *not* eternal torture. The redeemed will not have to listen to the screams of the wicked for ever and ever. We won't look across an abyss and see people suffering torment in flames, as in the fable Jesus told in Luke 16. The result of being cast into the lake of fire is *death*—the second death, eternal nonexistence. That's what Jesus came to save us from. Listen to the words of Jesus to Nicodemus: "For God so loved the world that He gave His only begotten Son, that whoever believes in Him should not perish but have everlasting life. For God did not send His Son into the world to condemn the world, but that the world through Him might be saved" (John 3:16, 17).

Whoever believes in Jesus has eternal life. And whoever does not will perish. I don't want to be one of those cast into the lake of fire. Nor does Jesus want you to be consumed by unquenchable fire. He longs for you to be saved. Jesus wants to write your name in the book of life. That happens when you accept Jesus as your Savior, and then you don't need to fear the sleep of death. If you should fall asleep in death before the return of Jesus, you will rise in the resurrection of the righteous!

## Reunion

I have come to know and respect a man of God named Dave Allen. Dave and his wife, Ginny, have devoted their lives to sharing the good news about Jesus with others. Some years ago, their son Bob died in a tragic accident after he was thrown from his snowmobile and hit a tree, chest first. Bob died at the scene, leaving a wife, two little girls ages 5½ and 2½, parents, and many other loved ones and friends. The pain of that loss seemed almost unbearable. Several days later Dave was driving over to visit his newly widowed daughter-in-law when a wave of sorrow enveloped him. He began to weep. As tears streamed down his face, he cried out, "O God, I loved my son, and he died on a tree!" That instant God spoke to Dave's heart as powerfully as if He were sitting by his side in the car: "I loved *My* Son too, and *He* died on a tree so *your* son could live for eternity."

That, my friends, is the good news, the gospel. It's not that life will always be easy. I can't promise you when you choose to follow Jesus that nothing difficult will happen. But I can tell you that He has the keys to death and the grave, and on that day when the dead in Christ rise first, there will be people looking for Bob. When you believe in Jesus, the sleep of death has lost its sting. Bob is not looking down from heaven, watching his family struggle without him. That would be a "living hell." No, he is sleeping in the sure and certain hope of a glorious resurrection when Jesus returns. That day will be a great reunion both for Bob's family and for all those who belong to Christ and have lost loved ones.

When you have accepted Jesus as your Savior, you don't need to fear death, either for yourself or for those you love—because Jesus holds the keys. "Do not be afraid; I am the First and the Last. I am He who lives, and was dead, and behold, I am alive forevermore. Amen. And I have the keys of Hades and of Death" (Revelation 1:17, 18). Allow Jesus today to become your personal Savior, and death will have lost its sting. You will live—*forever*.

# 8

## What Jesus Taught About His Church

"I don't need the church. All I need is Jesus!" Have you heard anybody say that? The statement is both right *and* wrong. Yes, Jesus *is* all we need, but those who love Jesus and accept Him as their Savior and Lord will not disregard what Jesus taught about His church.

The first recorded teaching by Jesus concerning His church appears in Matthew 16. "When Jesus came into the region of Caesarea Philippi, He asked His disciples, saying, 'Who do men say that I, the Son of Man, am?' So they said, 'Some say John the Baptist, some Elijah, and others Jeremiah or one of the prophets.' He said to them, 'But who do you say that I am?' Simon Peter answered and said, 'You are the Christ, the Son of the living God.' Jesus answered and said to him, 'Blessed are you, Simon Bar-Jonah, for flesh and blood has not revealed this to you, but My Father who is in heaven. And

I also say to you that you are Peter, and on this rock I will build My church, and the gates of Hades shall not prevail against it'" (Matthew 16:13-18).

In this brief conversation with Peter and the other disciples, Jesus shared four important truths about His church.

## Whose Church?

"And I also say to you that you are Peter, and on this rock I will build *My church*, and the gates of Hades shall not prevail against it" (verse 18). The first vital truth that Jesus shares with His disciples and with us is that He has a church, and He calls it "*My* church."

The word "church" in the Greek language is *ekklesia,* which means "called out." Classical Greek used the word for a political assembly, but the New Testament gives it special meaning: the *ekklesia* of God, the *ekklesia* of Jesus Christ. Those who are gathered together in the church that Jesus calls "My church" are the "called out" ones. What are we called out from? "But you are a chosen generation, a royal priesthood, a holy nation, His own special people, that you may proclaim the praises of Him who called you out of darkness into His marvelous light" (1 Peter 2:9).

## Called Out

When Kevin walked into my office about 18 months ago, he was living in darkness—or perhaps it would be more accurate to say he was "dying" in darkness. Kevin had been a functional cocaine addict for 26 years, but his junky world was now crashing down on his head. He had lost his wife, his house was going into foreclosure, and his creditors were about to repossess his SUV. About the only thing he had left was his life, and the cocaine was killing him. Although Kevin had known about Jesus when he was a little boy, he had wandered far away from Him and was living in darkness.

I looked straight into his bloodshot eyes and said, "Kevin, you need a miracle! Will you come to the House of Prayer, our weekly prayer service, this evening and ask the people of God to pray for you?" Having nowhere else to turn, he agreed to attend. That night he gave his testimony at the House of Prayer—not a testimony of victory, but one of failure. Kevin cried out to God for help. I asked if there might be present any men and women of God who wanted to pray for Kevin. I wish you could have seen what happened next. People came running up to the front of the church like a tsunami of blessing, surrounded him in prayer, and cried out to Jesus on his behalf.

I know what skeptics might say. "How can talking to someone you can't see transform a broken life and deliver anyone from the darkness of a destructive addiction?" I don't know exactly how it works, but I can testify that there is power when we pray in Jesus' name. Kevin was delivered that night! God set him free. Oh yes, he's faced a few bumps on the road in his walk with Jesus, His Savior. One Wednesday evening an old party friend gave Kevin some marijuana, but another friend was at the House of Prayer, and when he realized Kevin wasn't there, he felt deeply impressed to pray for him. Kevin was driving his van when he came under deep conviction. He stopped his vehicle and wrestled with God for about 15 minutes. Finally he crumpled the drug into a powder, started driving, and dumped it out the window. Today Kevin helps lead a Christian 12-step program at his local church, and he rejoices that Jesus has called him out of darkness and into His marvelous light.

The book of Revelation tells of a voice from heaven summoning the people of Babylon, "Come out of her, my people, lest you share in her sins, and lest you receive of her plagues" (Revelation 18:4). Jesus calls His people from the spiritual confusion of Babylon and into truth.

## My Church

Do you know why Jesus identifies His church as "*My*" church? Because He knew that others would try to set up their own counterparts. "Beware of false prophets, who come to you in sheep's clothing, but inwardly they are ravenous wolves," He warned (Matthew 7:15). What do such false prophets seek to do? The apostle Paul gives us the answer: "For I know this, that after my departure savage wolves will come in among you, not sparing the flock. Also from among yourselves men will rise up, speaking perverse things, to draw away the disciples after themselves" (Acts 20:29, 30).

Such "savage wolves" seek to establish their own version of church. They teach as doctrines human ideas instead of divine truth. So we need to be careful, because not every institution that labels itself "church" would qualify as the one that Jesus calls "My church."

## Still the Carpenter

"And I also say to you that you are Peter, and on this rock *I will build* My church, and the gates of Hades shall not prevail against it" (Matthew 16:18). A second important truth in the radical teaching of Jesus about the church is that *He* is the one who builds His church.

Some people think it's *their* job to construct God's church. It's not. Instead, Jesus asks us to join in what He is doing. He summons us to go into all the world to preach the good news about Him, baptizing people in the name of the Father, and the Son, and the Holy Spirit, teaching them to observe all the things that Jesus taught (see Matthew 28:19, 20). But even then we do not build the church. Jesus, forever the carpenter, erects His church! Notice the testimony of Luke about what happened at Pentecost: "And the Lord added to the church daily those who were being saved" (Acts 2:47).

Jesus builds His church. How does He do it? That's the topic of my book *The Radical Prayer*.[1] It's about Jesus calling us to join Him as He establishes His church. He invites us to give Him permission to involve us in His great spiritual harvest.

After the apostles prayed the radical prayer, Peter could boldly declare: "Therefore let all the house of Israel know assuredly that God has made this Jesus, whom you crucified, both Lord and Christ" (verse 36). His hearers came under deep conviction and exclaimed, "'Men and brethren, what shall we do?' Then Peter said to them, 'Repent, and let every one of you be baptized in the name of Jesus Christ for the remission of sins; and you shall receive the gift of the Holy Spirit. For the promise is to you and to your children, and to all who are afar off, as many as the Lord our God will call'" (verses 37-39). Peter exhorted them, "Be saved from this perverse generation" (verse 40). As a result of that powerful testimony about Jesus, about 3,000 people accepted baptism and joined the church.

Jesus was building His church on the day of Pentecost, and He continues to increase it today. You can experience radical joy when you join Him in His work! We have the privilege and joy of joining with Him wherever He needs us.

## This Rock

"And I also say to you that you are Peter, and *on this rock* I will build My church, and the gates of Hades shall not prevail against it" (Matthew 16:18). People have interpreted Jesus' comment in a variety of ways. Some claim that He was saying to Peter, "I'm going to build my church upon you!" A study of church history, though, reveals that this understanding emerged in the fifth century A.D., proposed by a bishop in Rome who claimed that Peter was the first bishop of Rome, and that religious authority passed down from bishop to bishop by a process known as apostolic succession. It ought to concern us that someone trying to consolidate his power and authority would advance such an interpretation.

However, a more careful look at the words of Jesus in Matthew 16:18 reveals something very interesting: "You are Peter (*Petros*), and on this rock (*petra*) I will build my church." If Jesus intended to build His church on Peter, He could have said, "You are Peter, and on *you* I will build my church." But Jesus uses two different words here: Petros— Peter's name—and petra—"rock." So what is this rock, this *petra*, on which Jesus will establish His church, if it's not Peter?

Such a question has two possible answers. First, this *petra,* the rock upon which Jesus builds His church, could be Peter's confession recorded just a few verses earlier: "You are the Christ, the Son of the Living God" (verse 16). Jesus could be saying, "I'll build my church on that rock-solid confession—'You are the Christ, the Son of the Living God.'" This is certainly a plausible explanation, but I prefer a second possible answer.

When Jesus says, "Upon this rock, this *petra,* I will build My church," He could have been referring to Himself. He uses this same word, *petra,* in His sermon on the mount: "Therefore whoever hears these sayings of Mine, and does them, I will liken him to a wise man who built his house on the *rock* (*petra*)" (Matthew 7:24).

The rock isn't Peter or any of those who claim to be his "successor." Instead, the rock is Jesus. The psalmist declared: "Oh come, let us sing to the Lord! Let us shout joyfully to the Rock of our salvation" (Psalm 95:1). The apostle Paul testified, "All [the Israelites in the wilderness] ate the same spiritual food, and all drank the same spiritual drink. For they drank of that spiritual Rock that followed them, and that Rock was Christ" (1 Corinthians 10:3, 4).

In fact, Peter himself clearly identifies Jesus as the Rock, the *petra,* on which the church is built. "Coming to Him as to a living stone, rejected indeed by men, but chosen by God and precious, you also, as living stones, are being built up a spiritual house, a holy priesthood, to offer up spiritual sacrifices acceptable to God through Jesus Christ. Therefore it is also contained in the Scripture, 'Behold, I lay in Zion a chief cornerstone, elect, precious, and he who believes on Him will by no means be put to shame.' Therefore, to you who believe, He is precious; but to those who are disobedient, 'the stone which the builders rejected has become the chief cornerstone,' and 'a stone of stumbling and a rock of offense.' They stumble, being disobedient to the word, to which they also were appointed" (1 Peter 2:4-8).

Jesus is the Rock upon whom His church is built. Some will reject Jesus. Refusing to listen to Him, they will stumble. But to those who believe in Jesus, those who understand that He is the Rock, He is indeed the "chief cornerstone" on whom His church is built.

## Binding and Loosing

What about the keys Jesus gave to Peter? What does that mean? "And I will give you the keys of the kingdom of heaven, and whatever you bind on earth will be bound in heaven, and whatever you loose on earth will be loosed in heaven" (Matthew 16:19). Some claim that it means that they have the keys to the doors of heaven and thus have the power to lock and unlock those doors. Perhaps you have seen pictures of a church leader holding such symbolic keys.

It does sound as if Peter received a lot of authority, doesn't it? But wait. In the center margin of my Bible it gives the *literal* translation of that text. It sounds a little awkward, but this is what the word of God actually says: "Whatever you bind on earth *will have been bound* in heaven, and whatever you loose on earth *will have been loosed* in heaven."

No person, no church, and no church leader has the authority to tell heaven what to do. The role of a true and faithful church leader is merely to confirm what God has *already* said. When someone comes to me, burdened down by guilt and shame, and confesses sin and asks for forgiveness in Jesus' name, I can boldly tell that person, "Your sins are forgiven." And that person *is* forgiven—not because I said so, but because God's Word says so. "If we confess our sins, He is faithful and just to forgive us our sins and to cleanse us from all unrighteousness" (1 John 1:9).

We simply confirm what God's Word has already declared to be true. So when a church leader claims to have authority to change biblical laws, but Jesus says, "If you love me, keep my commandments," we have to decide who alone has true authority in the church. Whom is the church built on? Is it a human religious leader, or is it Jesus, the Son of God? The answer clearly appears in the bold declaration of Jesus: "I am the way, the truth, and the life. No one comes to the Father except through Me" (John 14:6). Jesus declared, "All authority in heaven and on earth has been given to me" (Matthew 28:18, NIV). He is the one who has authority in His church. Not a church leader. Not a church council. Only Jesus.

## Prevailing

"And I also say to you that you are Peter, and on this rock I will build My church, and *the gates of Hades shall not prevail against it*" (Matthew 16:18). The fourth important truth in the radical teaching of Jesus about the church is that His church will be victorious.

Jesus gave this promise to us because He knew His enemy. He recognized that the gates of hell would *try* to prevail, that they would try to destroy what Jesus calls "My church." Not only did He give us this promise; He also provided evidence in His own life to prove that victory will come to all who are His. For example:

- Satan tried to destroy Jesus shortly after His birth. He failed.
- Satan tried to deceive, tempt, and bully Jesus in the wilderness. He failed.
- Satan tried to crush Jesus in the Garden of Gethsemane. He failed.
- Satan tried to overwhelm Jesus on the cross. He failed.
- Satan tried to keep Jesus in the tomb. He failed there, too.

So I can believe the words of Jesus when He says, "The gates of hell will not prevail against My church."

In the book of Revelation Jesus revealed to the apostle John some important details about the vast conflict between good and evil. "And war broke out in heaven: Michael and his angels fought with the dragon; and the dragon and his angels fought, but they did not prevail, nor was a place found for them in heaven any longer. So the great dragon was cast out, that serpent of old, called the Devil and Satan, who deceives the whole world; he was cast to the earth, and his angels were cast out with him. Then I heard a loud voice saying in heaven,

'Now salvation, and strength, and the kingdom of our God, and the power of His Christ have come, for the accuser of our brethren, who accused them before our God day and night, has been cast down'" (Revelation 12:7-10).

Satan attacks the church that Jesus is building. "For the devil has come down to you, having great wrath, because he knows that he has a short time" (verse 12). That sounds serious, but the apostle John tells us under inspiration, "They overcame him by the blood of the Lamb" (verse 11). They, that is, the saints—those who are called out, who keep the commandments of God and are faithful to Jesus, and who are part of the church that Jesus is building—overcome that old serpent called the devil or Satan. How? By the blood of the Lamb. What does that mean?

Revelation 7:14 describes the redeemed as "the ones who come out of the great tribulation, and washed their robes and made them white in the blood of the Lamb." Satan says, "You're a sinner and deserve to die," but the redeemed believe God's Word, which tells us "if we confess our sins, He is faithful and just to forgive us our sins and to cleanse us from all unrighteousness" (1 John 1:9). Satan says, "There's no hope for you," but the redeemed believe God's Word, which declares Jesus came to "save His people from their sins" (Matthew 1:21).

When Satan accuses you, you can overcome Him by the blood of the Lamb. You can say, "Get behind me, Satan. I belong to Jesus. My sins have been forgiven. I've been washed clean, and greater is the One who is in me than the one who is in the world."

The redeemed are those who count their relationship with Jesus worth more even than their own lives. John says of them, "They overcame him by the blood of the Lamb and by the word of their testimony; they did not love their lives so much as to shrink from death" (Revelation 12:11, NIV). The redeemed are not even afraid of death, because they know Jesus holds the keys of Hades and Death, and they refuse to be unfaithful to Him. The redeemed love Jesus so much that they are loyal to Him no matter what the cost. They love Him so much that they obey His commandments. Recognizing that He loved them first, they hold fast to the promise of ultimate victory. The gates of hell will not prevail against the church that Jesus builds!

Jesus is building His church even today—calling people out of darkness and out of spiritual confusion. He invites you to be part of His church. Make that decision right now. Respond to His invitation.[2] Then give Him permission to make you a laborer in His harvest.[3] There are people you know and love who need to respond to the radical claims of Jesus, and who must hear the radical teachings of Jesus while there is still time.[4] Soon Jesus will return. When that glorious day arrives, may you welcome Him with joy, and may many rejoice with you!

[1] Visit *The Radical Prayer* Web site at www.TheRadicalPrayer.com and learn more about a prayer that thousands of Christians are praying around the world.

[2] If you have responded to the invitation of Jesus and accepted Him as your personal Savior, I would love to hear from you. Go to www.TheRadicalTeachingsOfJesus.com, click on Contact Us, and send us your testimony.

[3] See *The Radical Prayer,* chapter 3.

[4] For resources that can help you to share the radical teachings of Jesus with others, go to www.TheRadicalTeachingsOfJesus.com.